T0311723

Parenting the Smart Kid

Parents of Smart Kids know they can have complex social, emotional, and intellectual needs. This resource condenses the wisdom and experience of teachers and school leaders who have experienced thousands of students with similar needs into 25 key tips for parents seeking to help their Smart Kids thrive.

Featuring 25 illustrated strategies for navigating situations unique to Smart Kids, with confident, informed support given every step of the way, this book covers topics such as:

- What to do when a Smart Kid thinks they are smarter than everyone else.
- How to motivate a Smart Kid who is bored of school.
- How are the Smart Kid perfectionist and procrastinator related? It's not all bad.
- How to navigate alternatives to regular school classes and other acceleration opportunities.
- Learn where to find valuable mentors in your community.
- When and how to act when the Smart Kid is too cool for school.

- What are the benefits and costs of homeschooling Smart Kids?
- Parents have great power in schools. Know when and how to use your power.
- What to do when the Smart Kid finally has a class that is not easy.
- And much more!

Parents are not alone on this complex journey. Take each tip and apply it. Watch Smart Kids thrive with an informed and confident parent.

Full of relevant tried-and-true suggestions that are immediately applicable solutions to the common challenges of parenting Smart Kids. This invaluable resource is a must-have for parents seeking to confidently navigate the exciting and challenging journey of their Smart Kid's teen years.

Brenda Kay Small is an author, trainer, presenter and teacher of graduate educational leadership courses for the University of Colorado and Regis University. She has served as a K-12 teacher and an International Baccalaureate high school and middle school principal.

Find training opportunities, her other books and blog at www.leadsmarteducation.com.

PARENTING THE SMART KID

25 TIPS NO ONE TOLD YOU ABOUT RAISING GIFTED TEENS

BRENDA KAY SMALL

Parents, explore these 25 Tips to learn from school leaders who share years of experiences on how to positively impact their Smart Kids at home, in school and into adulthood.

NEW YORK AND LONDON

Designed cover image: © Holly Brogaard

First published 2023
by Routledge
605 Third Avenue, New York, NY 10158

and by Routledge
4 Park Square, Milton Park, Abingdon, Oxon, OX14 4RN

Routledge is an imprint of the Taylor & Francis Group, an informa business

ISBN: 978-1-032-36594-7 (hbk)
ISBN: 978-1-032-36507-7 (pbk)
ISBN: 978-1-003-33281-7 (ebk)

DOI: 10.4324/9781003332817

Typeset in Futura
by Deanta Global Publishing Services, Chennai, India

Contents

Foreword

Gifted learners are often painted with a broad brush, but Smart Kids are not all the same. Raising resilient, productive, and thoughtful children takes deft parenting and the ability to change course as circumstances arise.

Raising my own four Smart Kids requires me to show up as my best self, even though three of my four children are now in college. The skills I learned from Dr. Small when she served as my children's middle school and high school principal have been invaluable as I've parented through their teen years. Dr. Small's advice and guidance enabled me to meet the unique parenting challenges my Smart Kids presented as they navigated their secondary education's peaks and valleys. This book is an extended visit to Dr. Small's office where she offers nuggets of wisdom and a toolkit for parents of Smart Kids to prepare them to better serve the distinctive needs of their children.

Dr. Small's tips for making school conferences and goal-setting sessions student-driven resonated with my Smart Kids. When I asked my children how their teachers and family best supported them throughout their school years, all four mentioned the adults in their lives having high but reasonable expectations for their performance and allowing them to have a seat at the table when making decisions that impacted them.

One of my daughters reminded me of a conference we convened when she did poorly on a math test in 9th grade. Her math teacher, Dr. Small, and the school counselor showed up ready to discuss her overall performance and how it had changed over time. The math teacher focused on brain development and how students learn mathematical concepts rather than how my daughter had performed in that one snapshot of time.

Under my daughter's leadership, we came up with a plan to have her work individually with the teacher and a tutor over the rest of the school year. She recalled that her takeaway from that plan was not that it was imperative to all of us that she get an A, but that she understand how the math she was learning was the foundation of all of her higher math classes. My husband said, "Even Tiger Woods has a golf coach," which made my daughter see tutoring as a way of mastering content instead of a punishment for getting a bad grade.

Reframing the idea that Smart Kids are always high achievers on every single assessment allowed her to get the assistance she needed to be successful in the math class and beyond. Dr. Small's approach of letting students lead conferences shaped my daughter's high school experience, and she will take the lesson to be willing to ask for help into the workforce so she isn't crippled by perfectionism.

Not all Smart Kids are overachievers. Not all Smart Kids are interested in the same courses, future careers, or extracurriculars. An important piece of parenting a Smart Kid is finding out what makes your Smart Kid tick. What are their special skills? What are their short- and long-term goals? What activities and courses excite them?

Dr. Small's *Describe This Smart Kid* questionnaire gives parents a tangible tool to get into the meat of who their Smart Kid is, how they learn, and how they interact with other people in and out of the classroom. The information parents gather from Dr. Small's questionnaire will paint a broader picture of what their Smart Kid is like apart from their role in the family and how to support their child as they pursue their own dreams – not the parent's dreams for them!

Finding and building communities for both Smart Kids and their families is Dr. Small's keystone parenting skill. Identifying your kid's "people" and yours is a vital lifeline for families raising gifted learners. Smart Kids recognize other Smart Kids. Smart Kids thrive when they are in class with other kids who are intelligent and have a wide array of interests. This tribe may not look like your Smart Kid in terms of socio-economic group, nationality, ethnicity, or area of giftedness.

A school setting where your child isn't always the smartest person in the room or the "expert" on something allows them to grow and recognize that each person they encounter can teach them something. Having parent mentors a few years ahead of you in raising a Smart Kid is essential to learn how to guide your own child and gives you an encouraging group of parents who know what it's like to nurture and support a gifted kid. The people Smart Kids surround themselves with often determines their high school path, from the extracurricular activities they join to the courses they take. Dr. Small's advice about navigating friendships and how to find supportive communities for you and your Smart Kid will help you establish a village for your family.

Dr. Small's expertise with gifted learners and their families was of great benefit to my family. Her willingness to be an empathetic ear and thoughtful advisor set many families at my children's schools up for success with the tools to nimbly navigate the school years with their Smart Kids. I'm thrilled that she's written this guidebook for parents of these remarkable learners. Her sage counsel will provide the scaffolding you need to build resilient, thriving Smart Kids!

Melissa Putnam

Parent of four Smart Kids

Chapter 1

Parenting Smart Kids: Do Not Act Alone!

DOI: 10.4324/9781003332817-1

Others might think parenting a Smart Kid is easy. What are they thinking? If this is the assumption, it is wrong. Parents are asked to hang on tight and navigate the bumps they see and feel daily.

Parents are alert of the differences and the unique needs of their Smart Kid. What are the right actions to take? When is too much or too little? The worries of the parent:

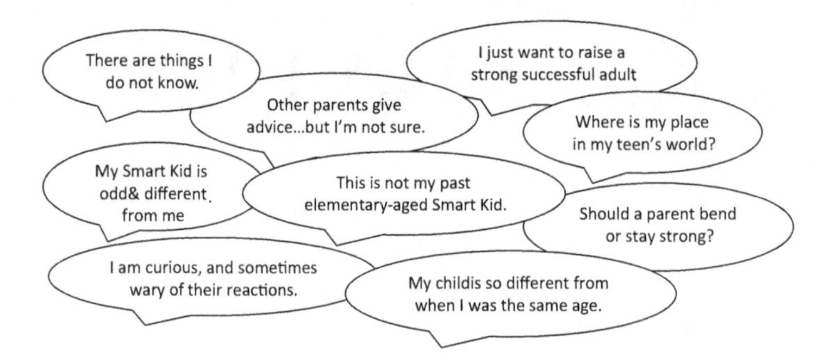

This book is written from a school administrator and teacher perspective. The years of noticing how students respond to parents and teachers, and more importantly, watching how parents respond to their Smart Kids, creates a wisdom that needs to be shared. These outcomes are written into 25 tips on trends and behaviors that are revealed as predictable with every year that passed in the administrator role. Teens are complex and change daily, even by the hour.

Read each tip and apply the wisdom. If one of the 25 tips is not applicable, wait a few years or even until the end of the week. It will soon be relevant to the parenting journey.

The push, the push back, the winner and the loser appear in front of school staff. Think about the wisdom gained by paying attention to these trends. What to do with the knowledge within them? These common trends or situations are obvious, clear, and right in front of the observant school leader. Sharing the wisdom gained from these experiences is a commitment to serving the positive development of children.

So, you are the parent of a Smart Kid. How is it going?

Parenting is complicated. So complicated that it exhausts even the most adaptable and conscientious parent. Smart Kid parents are called to take care of a child that seems to be two steps ahead of them all the time. Their child's IQ towers above their own and those in authority. The parent simply wants what is best for their child.

These 25 tips are from observations, experimentations, mistakes, and layers of professional experience in and out of the classroom. Think about the ratio of exposure to Smart Kids. A principal or teacher has experience with thousands of students. Parents have experience with one or two in their household. No, the school staff does not know the child as well as the parent when it comes to their at-home family nurturing – and schools are not meant to parent the Smart Kid. But school leaders and their staff are available to share notable experiences and wisdom gained through serving Smart Kids over many years.

Parenting practices vary in every home. What works today may not work tomorrow. Consider the practices that are relevant to diverse cultures and communities. The tips in Chapter 2 reveal lessons learned about how home life and practices can enhance the growth of the Smart Kid.

Communication, community, and citizenship give power to the parent in their child's school and school district. The tips in Chapter 3 showcase learned lessons in this area. Parents learn how they can actively use their schools for support in raising their Smart Kid.

Friends are a great confidence builder when a child feels different from their peers. Parents will receive information and encouragement to find their child's tribe. These relationships create a foundation of support for the entire household. The tips in Chapter 4 take the parent through the lessons learned on how to use others for support in raising a teen Smart Kid.

The road to high school graduation has so many twists and turns for parents... all parents.

Finally, check out the HACKs. These are immediately applicable solutions. No fluff, simply tried and true suggestions taken from the experience of the author, parents, and peers in the school system. Take note, the tips are written to reflect all demographics within schools and families. There is seldom a reference to gender, race, religion, culture, etc.

Enjoy the parenting journey! Utilize your village of positive, nurturing, and wise support!

Chapter 2

Behaviors in the Home

DOI: 10.4324/9781003332817-2

Chapter 2

Tip #1

So, your child thinks and acts like they are smarter than everyone, including you.

Join the club!

My son is 8 years old, 4 feet tall and acts like he has a PhD.

He claims he is smarter than adults. Every adult in his life.

The definition of a Smart Kid starts with a higher-than-average intelligence. This description is not related to age, culture, geographical location, or any other aspect outside the measure of intelligence. It is not a surprise that these children often have higher intellectual abilities than their parents, peers, professionals, etc. They know this fact very well.

This is just part of the picture of the whole child. Their high intelligence does not supersede the physical, emotional, and social immaturity of the child. So, the occasional outbursts where they correct adults are a natural phenomenon. That does not mean these corrections are acceptable. They are excruciatingly common with Smart Kids. Perhaps as common as the embarrassment of their parents…

Schools are filled with trained educators who have experience with the best and brightest. Some Smart Kids enter schools at the beginning of each school year with a superior attitude and the intent to take on the next grade level with brilliance and perfection. It takes savvy teachers and administrators to provide challenges for both their intellectual and their social and emotional growth.

This happens in every school that has quality programs in place to meet the needs of Smart Kids. A well-trained staff embraces these higher levels of intellectual ability, while nurturing the adolescent's social and emotional growth. It takes patience and an understanding of the reasons for their behavior. A sense of humor also helps.

There is a learning curve for new parents who suddenly experience this superior attitude from their child. It is best to start positive social coaching with this Smart Kid as soon as possible. These are gentle consistent actions meant to give the necessary tools to the child to thrive in a world of people with mixed intelligences. Encouraging empathy is a great place to start.

Parents step onto the path to success by recognizing the difference between mind, emotion, and physical maturity.

> *First,* acknowledge the child's unique giftedness verbally and often with positive encouragement.
>
> *Second,* explore (with the Smart Kid) the time and location of their verbal claim. Teach about social cues.
>
> *Third,* distract. Engage in short and lighthearted questions to move the focus beyond their current state of intellectual superiority.

Practice these steps in home-based situations. These steps are explored below with adaptable and easy to implement strategies.

Acknowledge and confirm the child's knowledge

Personality characteristics of Smart Kids include a heightened sensitivity to their world. They see everything as it is. There are few boundaries that impede their analysis of situations. Take this into consideration when coaching a highly intelligent child. They need your confirmation that they are correct. This is an easy action when the child is, indeed, correct. Say it out loud. Embrace their observation with compliments. Do not naysay their correctness.

Sensitive children who are mature for their age tend to be non-conformists. Their strong individualism should be praised as it leads to innovative thinking. By acknowledging that the child's spoken truth is correct, a parent continues to encourage creative thought.

It is understandable that not every situation is appropriate for verbal praise. Some statements that are obviously true when said in public should not be overtly praised. At a later and more appropriate place, acknowledge their claim and confirm their thoughts. Then take the important next step of pointing out proper public behavior.

Explore the time and location of their correction of others by teaching social cues

Bring the situation to the attention of the child. Ask them to consider the feelings of the people in the room or within hearing range. To build empathy, ask the child to describe how these persons might feel about the comments.

Address the child's insistence that the information was incorrect, and the adults needed to be corrected.

Walk through two or three alternative behaviors to the inappropriate behavior chosen. It is difficult for a sensitive and enthusiastic Smart Kid to not speak up to *right a wrong*. Simple questions may lead them to better decisions in the future, such as:

1. Is your correction of an individual going to *change the person's mind* about their own beliefs? If not, ask yourself why you are correcting them.

2. In a classroom, determine if it is *more important* to let the misinformation go and allow the class lesson to continue, or to correct the teacher. Consider talking privately with the teacher after the class.

3. Look at the situation and ask yourself *how the other people will feel* about you correcting this person. Sometimes it is better to let something go than to embarrass parents or others.

4. *"Feel" the emotions* of the person you are correcting. Is it worth upsetting someone?

5. Ask the person if you may *add to the conversation.* If granted, give the information as a fact or insight, not as a counter argument.

Polite social norms are learned in the home, school, a friend's home, a mall, club meetings, and even in online chats. Insist on the Smart Kid following the positive norms of the group. This is difficult because norms in a group of friends are much different from norms in a Sunday School class, or other groups. That is part of the lesson. Teach the importance of knowing the difference.

Polite habits to encourage

Maintain eye contact	Speak up, do not mumble	Listen before speaking	Avoid interrupting	Give cues you are listening like nodding	Open doors for people
Smile	No complaining without offering a solution	Avoid listening to and adding to gossip	Think before speaking	Remember names	Be alert to non-verbal cues
Treat all people with respect	Avoid bragging about accomplishments	Avoid judging others	Avoid swearing	Begin eating after everyone has their food	Practice light conversation topics

Model positive social behavior and alert the Smart Kid to take cues from the parent and to always watch and learn. Point out politeness when observed. A new sense of accountability may arise with this new "norm" of conversation. Persuade the child to avoid calling out others who do not engage in these newly learned positive social behaviors.

Distract... lighthearted questions change the smart kid's focus

In the middle of the heat of discussion, when the highly intelligent child is displaying the attitude of being smarter than everyone around them, appeal to their psychological need to be correct while taking quick actions to change the climate in the room without embarrassing the child or the recipient of their correction. This is a positive psychological approach that works if the parent can draw upon the child's true interests.

Transfer the focus to another topic, or come up with another creative solution. By doing this the adult is encouraging empathy while teaching alternative behaviors to correcting others. This takes a quick-thinking parent to get in front of a confrontation. Remember, the Smart Kid is often thinking in the abstract and analytically. Cater to their creative mind.

Lighthearted question examples:

1. Consider how the other person's information could also be correct.

2. The person you are judging is skillful in areas other than you. Can you list those areas?

3. What do you think you could learn from the person or people you consider your intellectual inferior?

4. How do you think that person felt about being corrected in public?

5. Besides knowledge, what are you learning in this situation – socially? Globally?

6. What are the societal concerns in this discussion?
7. How would you apply this knowledge or discussion to your future goals?
8. Describe the situation in which their information would be correct.

Test the learning with home-based situations

The self-motivated learner seeks to know everything they can find on a specific subject. Yes, this makes them an expert. As they seek to flex their intellectual muscles, use the suggested tools in this tip to refocus and expand their social and emotional thoughts. The parents of highly intelligent children have ridden this train since the child was a toddler. Their interests tend to shift soon after an immersion into a topic.

Each sequence of learning adds to the child's vast knowledge and interests. Their ability to remember and use this information is commendable and should be encouraged. It is that spark in their eyes when new information is discovered that inspires parents to keep encouraging their pursuit of knowledge.

Encourage this natural curiosity while maintaining social norms in their overt expressions. Model the list of polite actions with consistency. Use the lighthearted questions so often that the child can predict this part of your communication.

Not the smartest in everything

Exceptional abilities in academics does not always translate into exceptional abilities in other areas. For example, the student with straight A's in all accelerated classes may not have the ability to make a cake. Seek out opportunities for the Smart Kid to challenge their non-gifted side. These humbling experiences help to create a well-rounded and empathetic Smart Kid.

Celebrate that these exceptional abilities plus an adherence to social norms will serve the Smart Kid well as a highly effective adult in their future experiences with others.

Hack

Student: *"Check out this list of middle school clubs. I may be a joiner after all."*

Parent: *"You have to join a club or play on a sports team. Pick one."*

The benefits of joining a club or team are extraordinary for a Smart Kid!

Many are national organizations. Join or start a club in your school! Most schools only require an adult sponsor and administrative approval to get started! Ask a favorite teacher to be the sponsor and they will help get the process started. Just a few are below:

- Student Athletic Association
- Speech and Debate Club
- Film Club
- Environmental Club
- Future Farmers of America (FFA)
- Key Club
- Pi Club
- Anime Club
- Chess Club
- Big Brother Big Sister
- Mathletes
- Book Club
- eSports
- Habitat for Humanity
- Student Government
- World Language Clubs
- Thespian Club
- Health Occupation Society of America
- Photography Club
- Art History Club
- Academic Decathlon

Tip #2

My mind is all over the place…
Is that normal?
Middle school kids are just weird

Ask any middle school teacher, staff, or principal what they think of middle schoolers...

The answer is usually something like "middle school kids are just weird."

Are these common opinions in the home of a middle schooler?

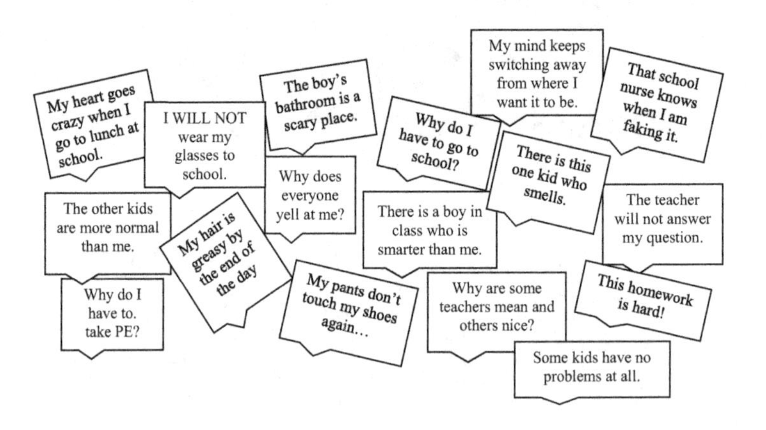

The same Smart Kid in middle school is different from when they attended elementary school just a few months earlier. What happened? They cannot be treated the same. During the summer there was an adolescent collision of physiological, emotional, and social dynamics.

Other parents are talking about it. A sibling may have transitioned easily, but this child has a bumpy path. Most teachers and parents advise you to listen, stay calm, and do not overreact to the high-drama conversations which tend to occur each morning and evening.

Recognize the changes taking place and verbalize them to the child. "I know you are feeling ______ right now. Let's talk about it." A listening ear and a safe and secure predictable home are the cure to most bumps in the road through middle school.

Are girls different from boys in this maturity process? Yes. A study conducted in California in 2019 found that both genders experience a drop in their academic self-efficacy during middle school. Girls experienced a substantial drop compared to boys in their belief that they can and will achieve good grades (Multon, 1991).

Why does this occur in middle school? The study by Multon suggests it is because of a new mix of children who are also Smart Kids. Students who attended the same elementary school for three or more years know the capability of their peers. A new environment is a new community of learners. Who is the smartest? The juggling of the social circle in the school is compounded by personal, social, and emotional changes. This is a lot for all 11- to 12-year-olds.

Positive academic self-belief generates positive outcomes (Multon, 1991). However, earning good grades in those middle years is more difficult. These obstacles to achievement have not been experienced in the past. Success in meeting past challenges is not part of this new picture. The adolescent must re-evaluate how to get that top grade.

Middle school kids are just weird

Even the brightest students experience these trials when going through this life stage. There are no quick solutions to skip the angst of middle school. Fortunately, there are several good practices that will help reduce the drama and lead to higher achievement:

1. Start in the late elementary years talking about middle school and how it will be different. Mention class changes, academic expectations, new students from other schools, teachers, hallway differences, etc.

2. Go to the middle school prior to attending. Walk the halls, go outside, experience the lunchroom, gymnasium, and classrooms.

3. Join social groups of middle school parents. Watch out for the Drama Mamas. Get to know other parents by talking in the elementary school car line, joining the parent teacher association, etc.

4. Volunteer at the middle school. This is important for parents. They will see that their own children are not that weird after all.

5. Set a strict schedule that is developed with the child. Agree on how important it is to follow this for bedtime, homework time, down time, etc. Keep to the schedule!

6. A parent's overreaction will be topped by the Smart Kid's overreaction. This is obvious when you see it. They are masters at emotional acceleration.

7. Stay consistent with everything. If it is promised, it is done. No exceptions.

8. Be available for conversations even when busy. Postponing a conversation at a time when a child is ready to talk will change the outcome.

9. Be present in the home. Just being around and not interacting is better than not being home at all.

10. Be OK with not getting in the last word in a discussion. Of course, the parent's objective is to always be respected. However, adolescents tend to grab a sliver of power with a quick, often unintelligible, word while exiting the room.

11. This is not the time to divorce, move, adopt another child, or otherwise upset the child's world. Of course, not all major stressors can be avoided. Just be aware that the impact on an adolescent is ten times that on an adult.

12. Listen to teachers and school leaders. They have chosen to work with this age group and have enjoyed thousands of experiences with them. Ask direct questions. Learn from their expertise.

13. Let the adolescent drive a car in an empty parking lot with parent supervision. Make this a distraction during an emotional spiral. Simple, but effective. It's adult-like and builds trust.

14. Embrace this age of the adolescent. It will only last a few years. There will be stories to tell when the child is an adult. Provide cautious support and constant supervision.

15. Parenting does not stop when your child reaches middle school (or high school). Now is the time to be present, alert, and questioning.

Adapted from *Serving the Needs of Your Smart Kids* (Small, 2022a)

Don't give too many choices... but give choices.

A direct order can be an invitation for a confrontation. Think ahead and give two to three choices. Make sure the parent or teacher is OK with any of the choices. This is simple but so important to a maturing teen. For example, provide a choice of buying one of three different types of shoes. They all fit, the price is similar, and they all look good. The teen gets the final say on which goes home.

Use this method with critical extracurricular activities. Will the teen be enjoying soccer, chess, or debate this year? They must select and participate in one club or team. The benefits are the same, teamwork, competition, friendships, personal growth. Let the teen decide then support their decision.

Teens often know which choice the parent wants them to select. They may select the opposite and watch for a reaction. Stay strong and supportive. This is a good training on decision making for the adolescent. They must live with their decisions, just like adults.

Refrain from telling the adolescent Smart Kid what to do. Give choices

- ✓ *Do you want to clean your room before school or before you go to bed?*
- ✓ *Chores for this week are your choice. Do you want to do the dishes or set the table each evening?*
- ✓ *Where do you want to do your homework: on the coffee table or the dining table?*
- ✓ *We are going to pick up dinner. Do you want to stay home and watch your sister or go with us?*
- ✓ *Grandma is coming over. Do you want to wait and go out after she arrives or return home early to see her?*

Control is a currency. Allow the teen to have control if they are making wise choices. Once the trust is broken, pull back on their choices and allow them to earn back their privilege of control. Give as much control to the child as safely possible. Then monitor closely and consistently.

A recent study asked adult Smart Kids where their support came from while in school. It revealed support mostly came from educators. Parents were second (Peterson et al., 2012). This information is important because parents should be aware of the influences on their children. Stay tuned into what is going on in school by being inquisitive, curious, and present. Balance the need to be involved without becoming too involved.

Tip #3

Relax! I am the smartest kid in class. Why should I try any harder…?

I am the best in class. The teacher and the other students know it.

I don't even have to study anymore to stay on top. Smooooth Sailing...

This tip concerns the Smart Kid who has reached the pinnacle of *their own efforts* because... they are the best in the class or club. The top has been reached. They confidently sit back and relax.

One of the outstanding personality characteristics of high-level learners is their focus on goals. This task-committed mindset works for and against the young scholar (Miedijensky, 2018). For many, if there is not another goal in place, relishing their already-met goal can continue long after it was reached.

Why this stagnation? Don't all children want to learn at the top of their ability? Yes and no. To get to their present success they had to work hard, focus on the subject, and explore different methods to accomplish their goal. They often work independently and master the goal before others. So, it is done. Some kids might ask, why push for more?

Clues that the Smart Kid is taking the easy way out:

✓ There are no books coming home. The response to questions about homework is, "I did it in class or at school."

- ✓ Study time at home is short. The child exits the study area and seeks out entertainment.
- ✓ Grades are high with excellent teacher comments.
- ✓ The child's friends are not in accelerated classes. There is little or no academic competition among friends.
- ✓ They frequently display a "this is good enough to be the best" attitude.

Signs the Smart Kid may not be in the appropriate classes or school environment:

- ✓ The child is consistently outranking other students in the class.
- ✓ It is obvious that having higher success than their peers is an expectation from others and themselves.
- ✓ They show signs of being capable of meeting the demands of a more rigorous class or assignment.
- ✓ The posted grades of assignments are all near perfect.
- ✓ The child consistently brags that they are used as a positive example for other students by their teacher.
- ✓ There is curiosity and frustration about why others do not achieve at the same level.
- ✓ In casual conversation, the teen frequently claims they are the "smartest kid in class."

✓ They complain that they feel different and that no one likes them in class.

Frog Pond Theory is ALIVE in accelerated classrooms

If a highly intelligent child is performing at grade level, does that mean they are underachieving? After also considering the social and emotional factors, the answer is probably "yes," though school experts have assessments to determine the actual academic strengths of students. There are many reasons for this lack of motivation. The underachievers may be simply trying to avoid attention. Know when to seek counseling for underachievement concerns.

Student groups have a direct impact on a child's learning. This is the social aspect, described by the Frog Pond Theory, which is a good visual metaphor of how groups behave. The class is the Frog Pond. There are students with mixed abilities and strengths. Their identification or groupings can be by grade level, gifted, differentiated classrooms, etc.

The best and the brightest are embedded into this classroom. The Frog Pond Theory suggests that placing a high-achieving student in the "pond" or classroom with average students gives the child two choices. First, they can work to be the best in the average class, only achieving "above average." Or, second, they can strive toward their personal best regardless of the top position in the "pond."

The first choice is made by the accelerated learner who wants to teeter at the top of the average scale and nothing more. They have won the top prize and relish their own brilliance. The second choice places the high-level learner into a classroom of average learners, yet they break down barriers to continue to make gains even after they have achieved the highest position in class. This is the preferred choice to adults, yet not the norm for teens. The second choice will make them feel different from the other students.

Parents can make the Frog Pond Theory work for their child by ensuring proper class placement. By learning with a group of high achievers, the student still strives to be the best. But, in this class the best has a high bar. The Smart Kid is in a pond of Smart Kids. Competition pushes learning up! Oh, the moans and groans will occur. But stick with it. Learning is happening.

Remember, the adolescent classroom is a petri dish of human emotions and experiences. Teens judge teens. Everyone knows who has the top grades and who is sliding. There can be peer pressure to keep to the status quo of lower expectations. Critical conversations must take place to find the reason a child is not trying. Bring in licensed professionals if needed to get to the heart of the reason for academic apathy.

School leaders and counselors may capitalize on the Frog Pond Theory for the benefit of a child's wellbeing. There are times when purposefully scheduling students into less rigorous courses is advantageous. For example, the student who has high core academics (Mathematics, English, and Science) may want a desired elective like Culinary Arts or Agri-Science. The team of supporters, including the counselor, gifted specialist, and parents decide placement. It may be best for the Smart Kid to experience this fun course in a different level of the Frog Pond to maintain a positive life balance.

What a difference a challenge makes in a Smart Kid!

Healthy challenges bring out the best in the Smart Kid. This is commonly accepted. Yet, the motivation to push toward high-level learning is more complicated because it is the child's choice (NAGC).

Accountability to respected and trusted authority figures is often all it takes to encourage higher goals. *"Come on, I know you can do this!"* This pure motivating confidence communicated to a child can break them out of an "above average mindset." Recognize the Smart Kid has the ability to stretch the content of a lesson. Provide supportive resources like online courses, museums, camps, etc. Be alert to the Frog Pond dynamics of ridicule or negative social pressure from others. Jump in and participate together in related extracurricular activities.

As a child enters higher grade levels, the challenges increase. What was easy to grasp in lower grades is now a challenge. This change is evidence of proper class level placement. Yes, there will be more homework and even the potential for a "less than perfect" grade. The young scholar must *learn* the material, not simply *study* the material.

There is a learning curve for adapting to more rigorous expectations. This is no longer elementary school. The student must learn how to learn, organize, juggle subjects, follow a calendar, and say "no" to more responsibilities.

Parents will notice a difference in a child's academic confidence. There will be less time spent on outside activities. Be patient. The balance will return once they learn how to manage these new academic challenges. Mastery of these skills is transferable to college and adult life.

Tip #4

Skip it, I got this, let's move on to something new...

"My child constantly complains about how easy his classes are this school year. He finishes his work much earlier than the other students. Grades are important, but I want him challenged."

Recognize these symptoms of boredom?

- ✓ Quickly grasps the lesson.
- ✓ Enthusiasm for learning is starting to leave the Smart Kid.
- ✓ Disengagement from school is leading to more interesting and less appropriate activities.
- ✓ Staying "off the radar" and trying to be ignored.
- ✓ Prefer to learn on their own.
- ✓ Asked to grade papers or do busy work until others finish a class assignment.
- ✓ Has the ability to answer all questions in class. Doesn't do so to avoid the social shunning.
- ✓ There is a manifestation of shyness, withdrawal from activities, and physical ailments.

Tips for managing boredom:

- ✓ Lessons are flexible to match a student's intellectual level.
- ✓ Opportunities for collaboration are provided for learning experiences above the current group's abilities.
- ✓ Listen to the details about their boredom with interest and provide solutions.
- ✓ Take school topics and delve deeper with field trips and other exciting activities. Include friends!
- ✓ Ask the teachers assigned to high-level learners for ideas on accelerations in the school, classroom, and community.
- ✓ Gather like-minded students and provide experiences such as museums, clubs, and other stimulating activities.
- ✓ Find online and virtual enrichment opportunities to expand on classroom learning.

Adapted from *Smart Kid Terminology* (Small, 2022b)

A few insights from educators on how thinking is different for our Smart Kids

Foundational skills:

It is assumed that all children enter a class with no knowledge or skills in the class content. This is not so for many high-level learners. There are Smart Kids who do not need to learn foundational skills. They already know, or understand, the basics. For example, a gifted child can achieve the correct answer for a math problem without working through the steps. They have the brain power to analyze and determine the correct answer without the foundational skills.

A well-trained school staff recognizes the need for this student to move on to a more challenging assignment. It is not preferable to insist the child go through the steps or repeat lessons on the foundational skills. This is a waste of their time and causes frustration. Parents are called on to recognize this issue and advocate for accelerated course content or another class placement.

The individualist as a high-level thinker:

The Smart Kid has the ability to see the world through a lens different from others. This vision creates a unique understanding of their world. Listen to the child explain their reasoning. This incredible gift resides between the lines. It is fascinating to listen to their "out of the box" explanations. This unconventional and non-conformist thought process sets the child apart. It is critical to fan the flame of this type of thinking. Suppressing it will lead to frustration, depression, and the hiding of their intelligence.

Parents build their child's confidence to express these unique opinions by listening and asking relevant questions. Encouraging self-assurance leads to safe environments where these free thinkers can expand their strong individualism (Miedijensky, 2018). By giving them space to be a non-conformist, children work things through themselves. They may come to the same conclusions as the masses, but probably not.

Intelligence plus creativity:

The Smart Kid's unique thinking skills foster both intelligence and creativity. This is a winning combination if the child is given room to explore. Well-trained teachers stimulate these strengths through active thinking lessons. Students may complain the teacher does not answer their questions. This is part of the learning process. The development of effective analytical thinking takes work and guided experimentation.

Parents can be alerted to a lack of adequate lessons through their child defining assignments as "busy work" which do not provide learning. Browse the lessons and assignments and look for indications that there is freedom to use individual creativity. Be aware of assignments with predetermined outcomes, rote memorization, or stale rhetoric.

Divergent thinkers:

Learning for high-level thinkers is a complex process. The dominant traits of creativity and intelligence pull together *every* aspect of their previous knowledge and their current environment to solve a problem or orchestrate a thought. This is characterized as *divergent thinking*.

Parents of Smart Kids recognize that their child will not always follow the set pattern of rules or norms. Their rationale takes them on a different path. They have "diverged" into another realm. Divergent thinking is described as a tendency to think outside of the box, use creativity, not take facts as given, and look to unique solutions to common problems. Convergent thinking, in contrast, is following a set pattern of thought (Edutopia, 2014).

The possession of exceptional abilities such as a creative imagination, extensive vocabulary, and an ability to recall facts *necessitates* a positive nurturing learning environment. Parents are highly encouraged to ask for properly trained teachers, the correct accelerated classes, and academic support from the school. Use parent power to ensure learning is taking place.

Remembering EVERYTHING:

Smart Kids have fascinating memories! Their parents have stories about how their 2-year-old could remember the route to the grocery store or how their 4-year-old could cite the dates of battles in World War II. Have these exceptional memories ever caused drama in the household? Yes!

These *above average long-term memories* are often the first clue a youngster is gifted. Family members may not remember the details, but the child remembers the exact wording, place, and time. Do not assume the child will have forgotten a promise made 5 years ago.

From the child's perspective, this memory can be overwhelming. There is an extraordinary amount of information saved in the Smart Kid's brain. This leads to that terrible feeling of being different from other teens and avoiding speaking up. Frustration occurs when others do not recall the same detailed information.

Parents should encourage individualism and offer tools for managing great memory:

✓ Recognize and teach social clues that indicate verbalizing a memory is not always appropriate.

✓ Embrace the child's differences. Identify and celebrate their great memory.

✓ Teach them to recognize others' limitations in recall ability in a conversation.

✓ Emphasize it is acceptable to intellectually compartmentalize information to bring up later.

✓ Teach the conversation skill of repeating facts to reset the memory of others.

✓ Encourage honesty and the importance of relating truthful facts.

✓ Stay alert to the negative aspects of a great memory in recalling past trauma. Know when to seek professional counseling.

Adapted from *Smart Kid Terminology* (Small, 2022b)

HACK

"These classes are too easy."

Have you already learned this material? Explore opportunities to accelerate learning in and out of school. The administrator has the power to allow students to skip classes in a progressive sequence.

Examples:

1. Taking college courses that are relevant to the high school graduation requirements.
2. Skipping the basic entry courses in a progression such as College and Career and World Language offerings.
3. Skip non-weighted 9th grade classes, going straight to 10th grade weighted classes.
4. Take core classes online instead of at school. This opens up time for elective courses in a student's schedule, which may add to their interests and increase engagement.

Tip #5

All the Smart Kids do this... So, don't make a big deal out of it (cheaters and liars)

How is work ethic related to high-level learners? It seems obvious that a Smart Kid enjoys an academic challenge. This enjoyment should lead to a purity in their attempts to solve problems and explore answers. Right? Not always…

So, where does work ethic come into a Smart Kid's journey?

Most Smart Kids are used to the feeling of success as they enter the secondary grades. They know what it is like to be one of the smartest children in a class. Their ability to understand the class content and go above the teacher's expectations is a staple in their young mind. Praise from authority figures is a powerful incentive to do well.

As the student enters secondary school, the playing field changes. There are more smart students. The teachers are less apt to praise. The Smart Kid's academic reputation has not travelled with them to the new school. Earning a place in the Smart Kid tribe takes effort. The social structure is different and demands navigation. This adolescent's emotions are pinging as their whole being goes through physiological changes at lightning speed.

Yes, it still counts as cheating if you don't get caught!

So, why not take a short cut to get the high grade? The workload has increased along with the intellectual competition. It is important to note that the motivation to adapt to challenges is the student's choice. The social and emotional changes in the environment do not take these choices from the student.

The calendar seems to drive the decisions to take short cuts. It is a pattern that teachers and administrators often see. First, the August and September months bring the need to get organized and understand the expectations of each course. There is an immediate demand to hit the ground running with assignments and learning the material. It is the child's choice to keep up or fall behind.

The next juncture of decision making is at the end of the first grading period. This usually occurs in October. Look at those grades! They are not what the child is used to receiving. It is time to make a decision on how to proceed. Does the child take the high road or the low road?

"But I want to be the Smart Kid like I was in elementary school!"

By the end of the semester, around December, the child is intimately aware of their own strengths and weaknesses. Their ability to complete rigorous academic assignments is now a part of their understanding. Good and bad. They realize what is demanded in terms of time and commitment for each class. Friends and family are experiencing this same understanding. This epiphany will drive the child's actions on how to proceed in the next semester and beyond.

At the end of the first semester the child is feeling the angst of giving up free time to keep up with rigorous assignments. Self-image takes a hit with that feeling of NOT receiving a perfect grade on a past assignment.

Underachievement is not the problem but a symptom (Siegle, 2013). Yes, this is where the "rubber meets the road" in deciding what grade they want to accomplish and how to get this grade.

Anxiety emerges. This is caused by a self-awareness that the child must change, adapt to the new workload, or accept a lessor outcome. Those around the child are questioning their abilities. This is a new experience for the Smart Kid.

To cheat or not to cheat?

The pressure is intense. The child is experiencing many tiers of stress including their own physiological changes. Their emotions are different from the little kids they were in elementary school. Their social circles have changed, which ramps up their anxiety. The work ethic of the past is not always enough. Now, they must change fast to keep up. The competitive nature of an accelerated learner cannot be understated. The pressure is real.

Short cuts look enticing. The conversations start between other Smart Kids experiencing these same emotions. Some are already making these less-than-ethical decisions and receiving top grades as a result. It takes little effort to jump into the cheating group. There are always methods to cheat. No teacher, school, or community can keep a child from cheating. It is the choice of the child to partake or not.

Schools and common consequences for cheating

Accelerated programs are a hotbed of competition among scholars. *Defining cheating with your child is important.* Addressing it outwardly and often is *important.*

Teachers work diligently to design assignments that make it difficult to cheat. Yet, the option to cheat is present in every assignment. The students are actually the "teachers" on figuring out how to cheat. Then the teacher has to change their assignment ... again ... to remedy this way of cheating. Many teachers of high-level learners create individualized assessments built around a child's personal learning. Group work is also a deterrent to cheating which maintains similar results in learning as individual assignments.

The consequences of cheating are stated in the beginning of the school year in every classroom, in schoolwide assemblies, and with notes sent home. These consequences must be relevant to the Smart Kid, i.e. have a personal emotional cost such as receiving a zero for all the students involved and informing staff and parents of the incident.

The teacher needs to have evidence of the offense, which will immediately be provided to the parents. It is common for Smart Kids to readily admit to cheating when caught. The common actions for cheating after the parents are informed is: first, the child who cheated and the child who shared their work both receive a zero for the assignment (Small, 2022a). Second, the teacher communicates the offense to all of the teachers of both students. Last, the incident is recorded. The consequences for subsequent offenses are usually suspension.

Tips for parents:

- ✓ Be unpredictable. Show up when and where it is not expected. Remember, the child has the ability to be two to three steps ahead of their parents.
- ✓ Recognize common buzzwords that may indicate a work ethic slip is occurring or is about to occur: *"she doesn't care if we share answers / everyone hates that teacher / everyone failed that test / she doesn't ever have time for me / she loses everyone's homework."*
- ✓ *Respect* information given by the child. Then, *inspect* the information. This takes little effort due to the parent's knowledge and control of the child's resources.
- ✓ State consequences for untruthfulness or misbehavior prior to an occurrence. Yes, there will be an occurrence. Follow through with the predetermined consequence EVERY time there is an occurrence. This method ensures it is the *child's choice* to misbehave and take the consequences.
- ✓ Set a precedent for supporting the school's actions when cheating occurs.

Adapted from *Smart Kid Terminology* (Small, 2022b)

Is lying normal?

Lying is frequently a symptom of avoidance. This could be as simple as not wanting to disappoint an authority figure, or as critical as a lie to cover up a direct defiance of a parental order. It is important to know the difference and deal with each appropriately.

Most children will stretch the truth to their parents at some point. They are experimenting with their power and independence. The parent has the responsibility to model truthful behavior at all times. Address the lying of others as examples of what not to do and why. Talk about why people lie and why they should always tell the truth.

Safety with adolescences is paramount. A child who is lying about their location or how they spent their money is a grievous offense. The social and emotional growth of a young Smart Kid is a whirlwind that frequently involves experimenting with different social groups. Know the child's friends by name. Be quick to call other parents for information that is both mundane (confirming assignments or events) and critical (is my child at your home?).

Address each lie as a lie. There is no room for "white lies" in a child's mind. It is either the truth or it is not the truth. Delve into the root of the reason for the lie. Ask the child why they lied. Ask the child to explain how they could have avoided lying. Walk through the scenario of what would have happened if they told the truth the first time. No, their world did not end. Always stress the importance of the parental role as their champion, supporter, and protector. Lying gets in the way of this role. Listen, then listen some more.

Tip #6

Where is my… oh, there it is… no, that's not it… ugh…

What is going on with this unorganized Smart Kid?

Where is my homework? I know I put it in my backpack.

Why do my folders have to be a certain color? That does not make sense.

Why spend time putting that in another place? It is fine where it is.

Some kids take too much time putting stuff away.

Why is this so important? It doesn't mean anything to me.

I don't have time to write a list. I just want to start.

Some Smart Kids compliantly follow established routines and habits created by authority figures. Others don't get it. Organization and routines are bothersome. Writing down lists or putting items in their place is not part of the schedule. The unorganized student does not meet deadlines and misplaces completed work, which reduces productivity and lowers results. Their fast-paced thoughts do not have time for such nonsense. The value of planned organization is not understood.

How can an innovative mind be stifled by these trivial actions to "put that away in its proper place?" Creative learning is messy. Look at high-performing accelerated classes. Students are grouped in classroom teams that are noisy. Their original thoughts are rewarded, not necessarily their compliance in putting away materials. To others, this type of learning is frequently viewed as noisy and unorganized. A savvy observer notices the embedded routines set up by the teacher in this Smart Kid classroom.

Parents of high achievers notice and celebrate the innovative bright mind. Yet the question "Where is my ____?" may occur hourly. This is a common frustration. Is there a connection between disorganization and a bright mind? Absolutely. It is the mindset of the child to continue what they are doing and not consider the peripheral expectations of organization. And why not? Isn't the objective to solve the problem?

Changing the Smart Kid's *mindset* to understand why organization is important is critical to personal growth. It is not an exaggeration to claim this is a key life skill. Teach through specific conversations, modeling organizational habits and patience. This will all cause noticeable stress. And a resistance to change. Point out these stressors when they occur.

Convince the Smart Kid to follow *routines*. This is like starting any habit. It is annoying and difficult to keep up. It takes days, weeks, and months to establish a habit. There are barriers, and many opportunities to retreat to previous unorganized behaviors. It takes watchful and encouraging parenting to make these critical habits stick.

What is going on in that brilliant mind?

The accelerated thinker has no time for busy work. The purpose of *this moment* is to solve *this problem*. Placing a paper behind a yellow tab as directed by the teacher is not important. It is a form of rebellion to avoid following organization rules set by teachers and parents.

The current intellectual pursuit or interest is the priority. Even personal appearance often takes a back seat as evidenced by messy hair and rumpled clothes. There is obvious frustration with rigid non-logical systems of organization.

This child is a visionary and looks at the big picture. The suggestion to stop and organize or write down an important due date is met with irritation. The unorganized Smart Kid has a lack of understanding and even a bit of curiosity about people who spend time organizing their space and writing lists. Calendars? Why? That is just more to carry.

How does a parent help a child conquer these unorganized habits while encouraging a love of learning? Use parent power to teach these valuable life skills. Start with the mindset then move to the tools that establish routines.

Conquering organization: It's a mindset

The brilliant mind is frequently distracted by trying to locate an item or struggling to remember a deadline. Organizational habits are tools that are used to help a child reach their full potential. Start with a frustrated child. This is fertile ground for suggestions of organizational habits and tools. Acknowledge the cost of time in disorganization.

Ask the Smart Kid to describe the good organizational systems of a person in their class. Discuss if this would work or how they would change it to apply to their needs. This is an interesting place to start the mindset change.

The location of specific items starts a habit of placement. Voila, no more searching. This takes time and gentle reminders. Even adults struggle with these life skills. Patience is pivotal. Next, introduce the luxury of keeping an up-to-date planner. It is an attitude, mindset, and mental exercise to use a planner. As teens enter secondary grades their agendas become packed with assignments and activities. Their classes become more complex with higher expectations. A pillar of success in accelerated academics is a good organizational system.

Conquering organization: It's a routine

The organization of the placement of items starts the routine. These are subtle tweaks with gentle reminders. The paper agenda is next. Write everything down. Experiment with different types of planners and duplicate written reminders like on desk or kitchen wall calendars. Writing in an agenda quickly becomes a habit once the student has had to use it to find critical information.

Stress can be calmed with predictable routines. Try not to vary the routine for days, weeks, and even months once it is set up. This means changing schedules so the child can be home at a specific time on a specific day to complete assigned tasks. The beginning of a routine is not the time to experiment with flexibility. Good upper-level teachers are masters of this concept.

Regardless of age, children thrive on set schedules for sleep, homework, meals, physical activity, meetings (such as tutoring), and organizational time. Watch and learn from the child. They will indicate when it is time to tweak or reorganize a routine. Dependable structure relieves stress. If it's working, stay with it.

Quick organizational tips

Always write due dates in an agenda	Color code class folders	Keep a calendar in a shared family area at home	Lights out at the same time every weeknight
Place backpack in same place every day (hook or table)	Keep backpack in order by color or binder	Take out homework after seated in class (ready to turn in)	Dinner at the same time every weekday
After school lazy time is OK until designated homework time	Keep extra supplies at home and school	Create a call/text/email list of classmates to confirm assignments	Tomorrow's clothes are out with backpack before bed
Keep sticky notes handy in backpack, nightstand, calendar to write down reminders	Write due dates in agenda as soon as the teacher gives the information	If on a block schedule, use a different backpack for each block	Think of school as your job. Use these employability skills to complete tasks
Stay alert by taking detailed notes during class	Use technology to enter dates and times. Use alarm reminders	Make to-do lists and sub lists. Enjoy crossing out accomplished tasks	Ask a friend, parent, or teacher to check organizational plan for accountability

HACK

"How can I be an organizer"

Here is how to start:

1. Create a list each morning. Cross off completed tasks.
2. Build and use a long-term calendar on the computer or paper.
3. Create a reward for the completion of tasks. Work toward the reward.
4. Make time for fun activities. Call it "me" time.
5. Be aware of and check the course syllabus or expectations.
6. Prioritize and schedule what needs to be done in the next hour, afternoon, or day. Be realistic.
7. Have a specific study spot.
8. Mornings are a great time to make lists and start those important tasks.
9. Have a routine schedule of study groups dedicated to specific subjects.
10. Ask a friend or authority person to hold you accountable to your plan.

Adapted from Course Hero (2022)

Tip #7

I'll pretend I don't get it, then I won't have to be so smart

It's over, I am done

There is daily pressure on the gifted child. Some thrive on the intellectual stimulation, while others burn out and want to rest. They want to get away from the world of the Smart Kid.

Why?

The enthusiasm for learning is gone. The Smart Kid is withdrawn and does the minimum amount of schoolwork to get the expected grade… if they choose to do the work at all. This is a different child than in previous school years or even recent months. What has happened to cause this shift in attitude?

A parent may know the answer. It may be an emotional loss that generated a feeling of "why bother to be better when tragedy is just around the corner." Or the cause could be due to a change in the family structure through divorce, marriage, another sibling arriving, moving house, etc. These emotional events are felt deeply by all children. Their energy has been exhausted on emotional stress. There is no room for analytical pursuits.

Parents may also be oblivious to the reason for the change. The topic can arise in parent–teacher conferences where the reasons are revealed. Is this the intent of the child? Perhaps. This usually occurs when the child's life balance is off. The Smart Kid wants their opinion to be heard by the school staff. They are looking for support – genuine support for *themselves*, not their grades.

Pressure from parents to keep getting stellar grades in all high-level classes becomes exceedingly difficult as multiple accelerated classes are added to their schedule. The time it takes to earn top grades at the higher levels increases tenfold from elementary to middle school. There is little time left for much-needed adolescent fun or rest.

Students who were not challenged in early grade levels may not have learned how to "learn" or study effectively. A strong work ethic was not established. Consequently, when multiple accelerated courses are added to a teen's schedule, they can reach a breaking point. The challenge is too much. The Smart Kid stops trying.

Interestingly, homework is often a cause for burnout over other reasons. It is often "piled on" for the sake of having homework. This busy work is a great irritant to the logical and pragmatic Smart Kid. Well-trained teachers who understand the gifted mind assign homework that matches a child's intellectual curiosity.

Teachers can be on the front line of this pressure. They want the Smart Kid in their accelerated class because they know they will do well and participate. Such intellectual exchanges in classrooms cause teachers to pursue these dedicated students.

A child who believes their success in school is the measure of their own self-worth may be rebelling against the system.

This pressure may also come from high-achieving peer groups who expect all their friends to be high achievers. It is concerning how quick Smart Kids can ostracize a former member of their social group who has sliding grades.

Self-sabotage is real

The student is in control. This is a fact. Parents and others have influence, but it is the child who chooses to change, adapt, or even listen. It is a choice to meet expectations as clearly as it is a choice to not meet expectations.

Proceed with extreme caution if a child's choice is designed to self-sabotage or self-harm. This is the ultimate form of control. Examples of harmful control are purposefully failing classes, disappearing, stopping eating, taking illegal drugs, changing peer groups, dating outside of their peer group, attempting suicide, or running away. Wise parents are watching and listening. They know when to change expectations and when to seek help from professionals.

Growing pains or too much pressure?

The tight rope parents must walk is clear: provide opportunities and encouragement for a child to grow to the height of their ability, but not too much pressure to break their spirit. Children are not smaller versions of adults. They see life through a different lens. Pressures are not adult pressures. Plus, the communication skills to articulate why they feel a certain way have not yet developed. Listen, then listen some more.

Acting out or, the opposite, disappearing into themselves is much easier to control than pushing back on grandiose expectations by authority figures. *See the child* before seeing the brilliance (or potential) of the Smart Kid. Embrace idiosyncrasies. Stoke the flame of a passion for learning. Downplay failures. Parent their adolescent mind, not an adult mind.

Get back in there... you can do this!

Accept the fact that the Smart Kid may not care or need to make the adults in their life happy. They are burned out working for others. A child's inner voice is louder than a family member's compassionate and rational argument against the stressor.

STEPS	**First**	Identify stressors
	Second	Provide management tools
	Third	Wait and support

Call out the stressor:

✓ Name it. Recognize these stresses are felt internally and emotionally.

✓ The child had a choice to "fight or take flight." This time they chose to "take flight." Find out why through good communication and better listening.

✓ Talk, listen, and listen some more. Start with friends, family and even teachers. How are their high expectations contributing to this attitude? What is causing the frustration? Listen and work to discover what is hurtful. Talk about the intentions of these support people.

Management tools:

✓ It is time for physical action to pull the Smart Kid back into trying. Ask the teen to write down their worries: list them, read each, and release their power. Journaling is a powerful tool to elicit self-discovery, gratitude, and goals. Words have power.

✓ Verbally walk through what is stressing the child. Take each element step-by-step. Talk it through until the end. Communication encourages strength and lays to rest those perceived dangers. Listen and learn what the child wants in their life.

✓ Let go of the fixed mindset of a Smart Kid having to achieve perfect grades. This is difficult, painful, but important to provide a purity of communication. The child needs to feel the parent has their best interest as a priority, not grades.

- ✓ Joy in a child is overt. It is obvious when joy is seen in a child's eyes. Find the joy in the Smart Kid's life. Work to include joyful events/conversations in each day. Natural talent is not always what brings joy. The development of a natural talent takes work.
- ✓ Jump into activities that demand creativity. This gets the brain working on solving problems, not creating them.
- ✓ Get them involved in a group. Sports, clubs, or other non-academic pursuits widen the child's self-image. This gives an opportunity to explore and find strengths unrealized and outside their high-achieving mind.

Wait and support:

- ✓ Establish purposeful groups of people with common interests, who are available to hang out with the Smart Kid in a non-stressful supportive arena. These positive motivators may be outside the usual peer group. Monitor conversations and outcomes.
- ✓ Give clear and non-biased options to release the Smart Kid from taking all high-level classes. Explore interesting electives that may not even be weighted as "advanced." Trade the higher GPA for a happy child.

✓ Support the description of the Smart Kid as a "hard worker" rather than a "gifted or Smart Kid" if this helps. This definition emphasizes that good grades and succeeding take time and focused work.

Academic success is not everything

High academics are not the only important aspect of a young Smart Kid's life. A study conducted by Pennsylvania State University interviewed adults who were in accelerated or gifted and talented programs in secondary school and found that balance is important. The value of social connections, family trips, and working in groups with like-minded intellectuals was the most important aspect of their own development. Positive experiences such as getting their driver's license or a fast-food job stood out as important to these high-level thinkers. Interestingly, these adult Smart Kids indicated that a balance of non-academic experiences made a significant positive developmental impact on them as adults (Peterson et al., 2012).

A word about bullying

A child who has changed from wanting to attend school to a child who wants to quit school may be experiencing bullying. Some of the signs of bulling are the expression of hopelessness, an aversion to previously enjoyed activities, social withdrawal, and difficulty sleeping or eating.

The common definition of bullying has three components:
1) Negative physical or verbal actions with hostile intent.
2) Conducted by a person of power / where there is an imbalance of power with the victim.
3) Incidents are repeated over time (Craig & Pepler, 2003).

Parents asking direct questions:

Have you seen someone bullied at school or outside school?
Tell me your definition of bullying.
Have you ever been bullied?
Have you seen another child be threatened by anyone?
Tell me about how bullying can be non-physical.

Parents asking open-ended questions:

Tell me about lunch.
What happens after school?
Who do you see in the hallways?
What happens in the locker room at school?
Who would you consider a mean person at your school?
What do the school staff tell you to do if someone is bullied?
What are your feelings when you are on your way to school?

Adapted from Jung et al. (2022)

Tip #8

Perfectionists and procrastinators – Normal for a Smart Kid?

All the Smart Kids do this.... so, don't make a big deal out of it.

Is this the conversation starter at home? How is a parent to know which Smart Kid behaviors are a concern? There are other parents and teachers to talk to, yet every child is different. Alas, they are different from one day to the next.

What to believe? Is this really a crisis? When should a parent act?

When does a parent just "chill" and let the Smart Kid grow independently?

The content in this tip is taken from experiences with thousands of Smart Kids, their parents, and teachers. Much of this wisdom was learned from the parents of graduates and adult Smart Kids. Remember, teens live in a storm of emotional, intellectual, physiological, and social change. When there is finally more balance in their world, they can accurately reflect on those tempestuous teen years.

Parents listen. This is the first response. Wait for key words indicating the child's feelings on the issue. Relate personal experiences or simply nod to keep the dialogue going. Stand back and watch as the Smart Kid takes their own steps to solve the issue. The parent sees the "cliff" approaching. Yes, there it is, and the child is moving toward this impending doom. Be patient and watch. Will the child make a move to avoid "the fall" or will there be a tumble? *Of course, if safety is a concern, the parent always catches the child.*

When a lesson is waiting to be learned, there are two paths to take. The first path is the child's avoidance of falling from the cliff by trying and succeeding in learning the lesson even if they stumble: celebrations occur. The parent claps, yells praises, yay you! If the second path is taken, the parent's kind support stops the child from falling or stumbling down the cliff. The child is grateful, maybe silently. A lesson may not have been learned. Any irritation is from the Smart Kid's disappointment in themselves. Deal with the consequences of the fall: the success or the save. This method respects the Smart Kid through patience and organic learning.

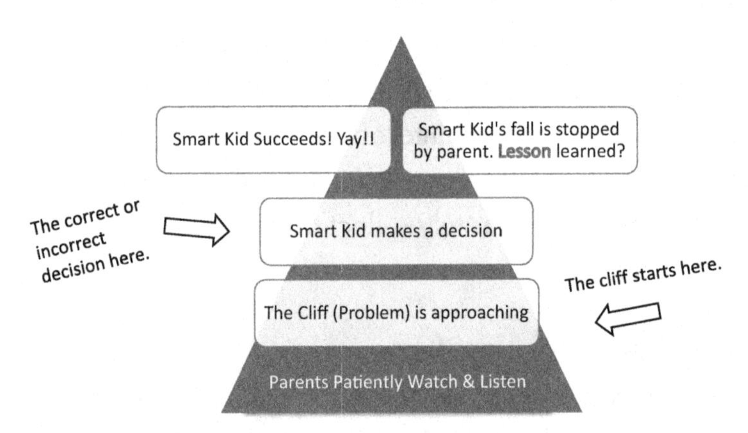

Apply this cliff analogy when asking the question if procrastinators and perfectionists are normal or if they are related.

Procrastinators

Smart Kids are known to often put the "pro" in procrastination. The fact that this is normal rarely makes a worried parent feel better. The type of procrastinator is important to notice. The first type will meet the deadline. The second type will not meet the deadline. In general, the Smart Kid will meet their deadlines.

Why do bright children wait until the last moment to complete a task? One reason is that Smart Kids pile too much on to their plates: vast responsibilities and commitments to others. The list of tasks is lengthy with every numbered item a priority. Interestingly, by waiting until a due date is critically close, the Smart Kid is forced to prioritize their time. That's it! Now it is a priority. Intellectual energy can now be focused on that prioritized task.

Procrastination is a tool to sort priorities by time.

The high-level learner rarely uses "having fun" as an excuse for procrastination. Their reasons for procrastination are more task-centric in meeting other deadlines. Of course, the quality of the work may be in question. Yet, it is completed and turned in. The frequent impending catastrophe of common deadlines glare in the vision of the watchful parent.

Watch, listen, and provide a safety net for the cliff.

Model non-procrastination behaviors by communicating how to set daily goals on tasks with future deadlines. Procrastinators have a knack of holding a family hostage. This interruption is not allowed. The pressure created by the Smart Kid is on them, totally on them and not the family, classmates, or teacher.

Let the procrastinator feel it. Oh, it hurts. Learning life lessons can be painful.

Brainstorm strategies with the Smart Kid and find a system that works. This is their solution, not the solution of the parent. Suggestions can include writing down a short list of daily goals each morning, posting calendars, crossing off completed tasks, celebrating early completions, etc.

Smart Kids already feel different from other children and even their siblings. By highlighting the positives and supporting them in dealing with *what they consider* the negatives, a parent will be nurturing a well-adjusted and confident child. Work from procrastination toward rational decision making.

In time the child will take on the next cliff, or problem, with a less stressful solution.

Perfectionists

This mental and emotional trait is simply defined as a person who refuses to accept any standard short of perfection (Oxford, n.d.). The perfectionist is related to the procrastinator. Leaving a task until it can be the sole focus allows the perfectionist to make the work perfect. Parents of perfectionists must endure the frequent intensity of both celebrations and emotional breakdowns.

This personality strives for flawlessness in every endeavor. Less than perfect is not acceptable. Period. These impossibly high expectations or standards for their own accomplishments often generate a self-imposed crisis that leads the Smart Kid towards the cliff.

All parents want their child to try to do their best, but when is it enough? This is a tight rope.

Not everyone receives a trophy. Or, more poignantly, the experience of childhood must include the feeling of failure. Why? Because it happens. But the perfectionist works diligently to avoid failure. This work includes keeping control, not participating, avoiding non-expert tasks, etc. This is the moment the child arrives at the cliff. Remember to watch and listen. Is this the time to allow the child to experience failure (or the child's perception of failure)? Or is this the time to catch the child and create a situation of success?

What to do?

Perfectionism can be considered both a negative and a positive trait. (Hamachek, 1978). There are two types of perfectionism that lead to this view: *normal* and *neurotic*. The Smart Kid may have both types. A *normal* perfectionist receives edification from organized success and is motivated to work diligently to achieve established goals. Failure is not the end of the world. Lessons are learned. The *neurotic* perfectionist sees deficits in even the most brilliant work. Failures are felt personally and held as a reflection on their weaknesses (Small, 2022b).

A parent's unwavering commitment to watch and listen can determine the type of perfectionism their child has. The Smart Kid who has experienced a past failure should adapt and learn from their mistakes. This healthy perfectionist seeks out organization strategies, more time practicing a talent, and support.

Mental energy is put into the effort needed to meet their own high expectations. Too high?

The child who is making poor decisions at the cliff edge alerts parents to a possibly unhealthy perfectionist personality. Parents need to intervene if their Smart Kid is showing overt anxiety. This stress can be established through the child's predicted failures, inaccurate preparations, peer competition and even perceived parental expectations.

Expected criticism of their failure can be a disabling fixation for them. Watch out for this!

The negative aspects of a perfectionist child often bubble up in parent conversations, student conferences and when supporters are involved in the child's current crisis. It is wise for school staff to keep an eye out for the two types of perfectionism when engaging with families. Parents are encouraged to recognize the difference between the two types of perfectionists and take positive actions toward nurturing their child.

Perfectionist behaviors do not go away.

A child knows when they have the support of their family and school. Make sure the Smart Kid does not take advantage of this situation. Remember they are probably the smartest one in the equation. The "soft place to land" for the Smart Kid does not change their opinion of the child because of choices they make.

Here comes another cliff, and another…

Tip #9

Six traits: Chronic overthinker, imposter syndrome, isolation by choice, multiple exceptionalities, intensity, sensitivity

Who are these Smart Kids and why do their teachers relate to them so well?

Parents often experience unfamiliar behaviors in their children that they deem odd. This tip is a gathering of common Smart Kid behaviors often addressed by experienced professionals in schools. The veteran teacher of accelerated learners recognizes these traits and deals with them instinctively without needing much input from parents. Now is the time to jump into their meanings and remain as informed as experienced Smart Kid teachers.

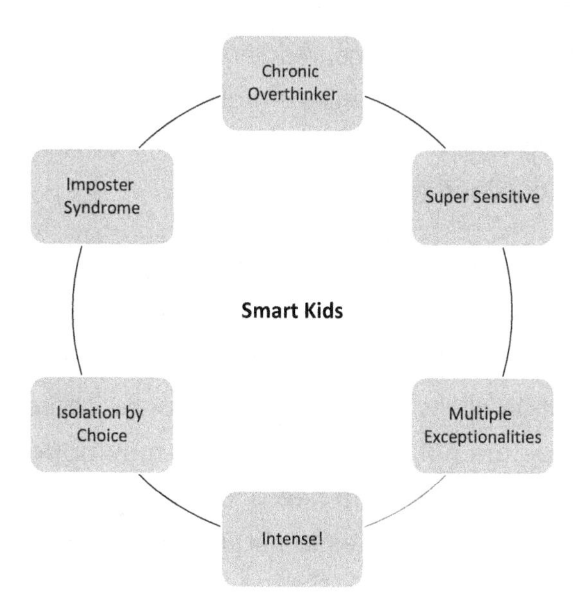

Just growing pains or too much pressure?

The quest for reasonable balance in a Smart Kid's life exists in homes and schools everywhere. Most of us have heard this phrase often: children are not smaller versions of adults. They experience life differently. They are in the middle of a storm of changes from their bodies to their minds. Sometimes it can seem like a stranger is in the home. It may help to understand them by learning about some common traits among Smart Kids. These traits are not exclusive to the brightest children. They are felt by many teens and adults.

Recognize that the pressures in their world are felt with intensity. These Smart Kids are experimenting with coping tools. Not all will be successful. These traits are embedded into their quest for balance. Additionally, their undeveloped communication skills sometimes make it easier to not speak to inquisitive adults. Nurturing parents and advocates will seek to understand these idiosyncrasies.

The learning environment gives young intellectuals a safe place to compare their strengths to others. Sometimes these are positive comparisons, sometimes negative. Each situation elicits an emotional response. Learn these traits. If they are not relevant now, they may appear at any minute. The Smart Kid needs knowledgeable and supportive family structures to nurture this balance.

Chronic overthinkers

Parents will notice overthinking in their child's inability to take a situation or problem at face value and move on to another topic. Such *analysis paralysis* is often enjoyed because the child likes the analytical exercise. Not dropping the problem is the problem. The Smart Kid is so engrossed in the analysis that they cannot shake it. Parents notice that every conversation must evolve into a verbal analysis and discussion of this problem.

Overthinkers analyze all aspects of their world and predict problems. *They see the trees and not the forest in most situations.* They delight in exploring minute details and the plethora of possible solutions. This literal thinking and overt communication are considered highly important. The Smart Kid is so obsessed with an idea that mundane tasks like bathing, finishing homework, or playing outside are not even a consideration.

Part of this trait comes with a learning style that expresses itself as a need to know all the reasons or all the details of a project. Social costs are cast away as unimportant when the Smart Kid knows the answer and calls it out regardless of the situation. There is also a tendency to openly correct authority figures when details are not accurate. Understand that this behavior is not chosen so the child can be a star, it is chosen to get the correct information out as soon as possible.

Supportive parents gently point out the situation and why it is a benefit to move on. Or more bluntly encourage the adequacy of a surface understanding. Such a redirection of energy is a strategy often used in classrooms. Children are encouraged to turn their attention to another activity they enjoy. Consider this an escape out of the analysis paralysis.

	Chronic overthinker strategies
1	Realize the world often places limits on intellectual input.
2	Light work, exercise, or working on a hobby deflects overthinking.
3	Knowing all the answers: give the most common first, save the others for another time.
4	Combat analysis paralysis by embracing one answer and moving on.
5	Conformity reduces stress. Stay with the pack.
6	Physically change the environment and seek other senses to shake the thoughts.
7	Find practical distractions from the thoughts. Jump into another activity.
8	Write deadlines with completion times to reset the mind to focus on the next item.
9	Take a mountain top view. Pull back from the details at ground level to shake the trance.
10	Put yourself into the listener's role. Do they want to hear more? Think about it.

Adapted from *Smart Kid Terminology* (Small, 2022b)

Imposter syndrome

"I should not be here. I am a fraud. I am not as smart as I used to be.

What are they talking about? They are going to find out I don't know this stuff."

Experiences of intellectual self-doubt are felt in some kids with a panicking sense that they are not adequate and do not belong in their environment. Imposter syndrome often occurs in new situations. Smart Kids experience insecurities in their ability to succeed or even try.

It seems obvious the perfectionist is the most likely to feel this syndrome when confronted with a new task. It is a social disadvantage to unmask these perceived weaknesses to others. This heightened sensitivity often leads to self-isolation and an avoidance of communicating the issue to authority.

Some Smart Kids attribute their successes to luck. This syndrome is a result of insecurities in their learning abilities. This lack of confidence may also be a manifestation of external pressures from family, coaches, school staff, or peers. Additionally, students of minority or diverse backgrounds often experience feelings that they do not belong. Especially if they are unique among their classmates or group.

Overcoming impostor syndrome takes time, acknowledgement, and the experience of growth. Parents are encouraged to openly communicate if they see their child exhibiting signs of this syndrome. Describe the child's strengths that can be applied in this new situation. Explain how others may have similar feelings.

Celebrate how new activities are challenges and not threats. Parents model embracing their own challenges and recognizing small personal progress. Take the child's words used to describe their concerns with great care. This trust in their parents to understand and offer support is critical in gaining the confidence to excel.

Smart Kids are very likely to feel impostor syndrome at some point in their young lives. This is part of their high intellectual complexity related to their need to learn and challenge themselves. Learning to adapt to new environments with the confidence to learn is the only way to deal with it. Each occurrence is another lesson in confidence.

Parents are called to assist their children in embracing their differences. This means children are not expected to be perfect at every task every time. Every gain made is an achievement. Mastery is not always possible for Smart Kids.

Isolation by choice

Is it acceptable for children to spend hours alone?

Is this just a need to "reset" from the daily academic and social pressures?

How much is too much time alone?

Parents compare their Smart Kid to others their age who enjoy socializing with friends. Yet, their child chooses to spend time alone. This is a concerning behavior.

The answer is, no. It is not acceptable for teens to be alone for hours. Isolation is a habit. It takes purposeful and creative parenting strategies to move a child out of this cycle. Remember, even at a young age, a bright child can accurately predict parental behaviors. Their world of isolation may be aggressively protected. The Smart Kid will be one step ahead of their parent and ready to argue their side of keeping to their isolation.

The reason for isolation is commonly stated as "I don't fit in so it's easier to be alone." A child who feels like a misfit finds solace in their intellectual pursuits where they can be themselves without judgment. Frequently, the peers of highly intelligent children are not the same age. There is no common intellectual understanding of a beloved hobby or subject. Others just do not understand. This brings little joy in speaking with peers.

This alone time may be unpleasant for a child. The computer can get hours of attention as friends are neglected. Consider learning more about internet addictions. The child may feel they have no other choice. Parents are called on to provide better choices.

Is there a positive side to self-isolation? The answer is yes, but with caveats. This time may be considered a recharge or reset time. This is time without interruption for introverts to think, which can produce creative thoughts. A Smart Kid may express their motivation to be alone as a motivation to learn and explore. This is a solo task. There is no need to involve others.

Open a dialogue on the reasons for isolation. Observe and be alert to any changes in routine leading to withdrawal from family and friends. Be persistent in the exploration of the child's perceived problems. Always provide options of solutions in a way the child will welcome.

Encourage activities with like-minded Smart Kids. Ideas should be generated after listening to the child's opinion on their possible interests. These are the child's interests, not necessarily the parent's interests. Start slow and gently encourage interaction. Look outside the child's age group and shift the focus to common interests.

Multiple exceptionalities

There is an *exceptional ability in one area* and a perceived inability in a different area. An example of a person who is Twice Exceptional (2e) is Stephen Hawkins. He could not speak or walk, and he was a brilliant physicist. Another example is Stevie Wonder. He is blind, yet a masterful musician and pianist. They both have physical exceptionalities. There are cognitive and behavioral examples too. A brilliant child may have difficulty with social situations due to a past trauma. A brilliant reader may not be able to write. A math genius may not have the ability to read.

> *"Parents can serve as advocates for their 2e child by knowing their child's strengths, weaknesses, and learning style. In an ideal world, a child's learning style matches the classroom experience, so it's*

> *important to be well-versed in your child's profile to help inform the teacher and school." (NAGC, n.d. b)*

Dual Exceptionality is another common term for the same trait. A child may earn this designation through having significant gaps between performance in schoolwork and their performance on tests. These developmental challenges are commonly accompanied by high intelligence.

Perfectionism is the enemy of a 2e Smart Kid. This self-induced frustration is a block to multiple learning tools that help adapt to exceptionalities. Losing confidence and negative self-talk are to be dealt with immediately. Watch carefully, Smart Kids are masters at masking learning problems by using their strengths to compensate for their weaknesses.

Parents are key advocates for children with multiple exceptionalities. Their role is to provide a positive nurturing home that discovers tools to encourage a child with 2e to learn and perform at their highest level. Active parents and the child's advocates play a significant role in recognizing they are 2e. Know what the child needs and ask for it.

These are Smart Kids. Empower them by celebrating their strengths. Identify their challenges with a quest to improve. Parents should purposely keep the lines of communication open with specific praise and encouragement, especially when a task is difficult. Encourage the exploration of the child's own learning styles. These may be spatial, kinesthetic, auditory, visual, etc.

Don't be afraid to accept a child's differences as uniquely theirs. A parent's encouragement has the power to make a child believe they can conquer the academic world. Young minds require a balance in the child's world to function. Watch as they grow exponentially under the careful guidance of their advocates who understand their needs.

That is so intense!

There is the saying "wearing our emotions on our sleeve." That is what intense Smart Kids do. They express themselves with an energy that could power a light bulb. Often referred to as "overexcitability," this is a heightened awareness of one's environment.

Parents know it when they see it. Overt feelings felt with extreme all-encompassing emotions. The gentle description is that "my child is a sensitive person." This description does not come close to the intensity of the emotions felt by these Smart Kids.

The intense child has a vivid and active imagination. They see all possibilities at the same time. This often manifests into fears about the future, anxiety, and debilitating phobias. Parents experience the sensitive child's response to world events such as the state of the environment or governmental issues. These intense Smart Kids know critical details and frequently do not understand why the adults in the world do not take immediate action.

Moral issues and social justice are also at the forefront of their minds. Overexcitable children often adopt causes and seek to solve problems. Their deep empathy for others is often targeted at outcasts, underrepresented youth, and people living in poverty.

Make sure home is a safe place to express intense emotions. If not, this will happen in a public or school setting. A parent can generally predict the next emotional event. It is coming. Be ready with patience and a toolkit for both the parent and child to manage it. *Feel it. Identify it. Accept it.* This intense personal emotion is part of the family fabric. The response should never be "just relax" or "you are overreacting, calm down."

As always, listening to the Smart Kid with overexcitability is a positive place to start. Let the child talk about it with their own words and expressions. The family home or car should be a safe place to feel these emotions without the fear of judgment from others.

A parent attempting to suppress these heightened emotions is usually due to frustration, and will end in failure. Always ask questions that lead to the emotions winding down, such as: "And then what happened? What do you think will happen next? Has this ever happened before? When will this happen? What can you do to help? Have you written down your thoughts? Who has the power to change this? What is our next step?" That is an intense conversation.

A fellow intense Smart Kid may be the ticket to success. Find and nurture relationships with children, or even adults, of similar interests and intensities. This group compassion is not only fun to watch, but the Smart Kids may work together and solve an important problem.

Deep feelings and the sensitive Smart Kid

The sensitive Smart Kid is similar, but different, from the intense child. The child with acute sensitivity draws emotions from inside themselves. These are emotional responses to their environment. It is common for the child to know they are different from others. They frequently question why others are not bothered by a situation. For them it is personal.

This sensitive child's response is quick and heartfelt. A negative word or action from another person is not ignored as easily as by peers who have no problem negating the issue and moving on. They often feel misunderstood as they explain to others why they need to react… immediately.

The sensitive Smart Kid

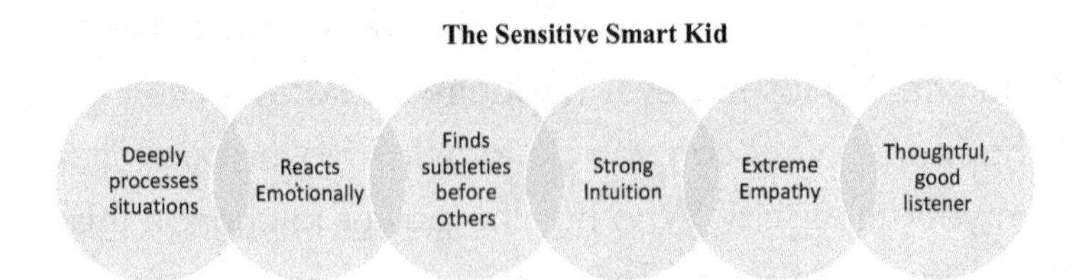

It is common for physical manifestations of feelings to occur. This may look like a stomachache, headache, heart racing, IBS, sweating, etc. Parents should react to these symptoms with calm and concerned communication about the issues. Making the child feel safe and secure is the first step.

A typical reaction to a person's sensitivity is a lecture on being less sensitive and to stop overreacting. *This does not work.* The Smart Kid knows that parents, teachers, and peers are trying to quell their feelings. Their sensitive feelings are then compounded by their fight for justice.

Parents can understand where the child is at in their thoughts by providing an instrument to measure their feelings. Ask the Smart Kid to scale their emotions from 1 to 10. Is the intensity a 2 or a 9? Start with the number given by the child and work toward lowering the intensity to a 1. Discuss how they feel and why. Visually walk through each step of the situation. Listen to the concerns and beliefs. Treat each with compassion. Keep the conversation positive.

Discuss the bigger picture with the Smart Kid. Determine if others are causing an issue. This could be the media, peer groups, bullying, etc. Sometimes it is difficult to shield your child from certain outside influences. There are social and societal pressures to keep their opinions locked inside their emotions. Are people in the child's life relating exaggerated or untrue negative facts? Have frequent conversations that last as long as the child needs to talk.

Tip #10

Feeling depressed, stressed, not good at anything. Burnout!

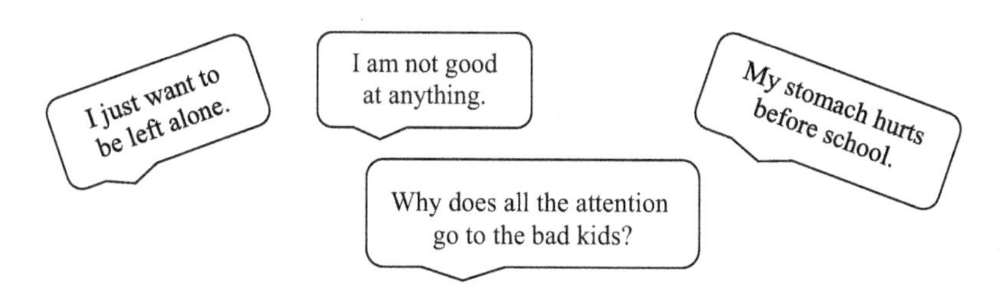

Parents of Smart Kids may have heard comments like these from their child. Most teens go through emotional highs and lows. This comes with the territory as they navigate the social and emotional changes in their world at that age. *They are a different person from the elementary child they used to be.*

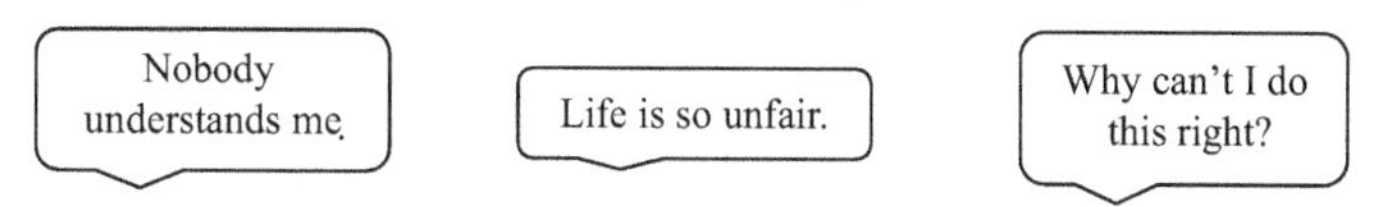

There may be unrealistic expectations of their own abilities in a new environment. This perceived failure of not meeting these expectations makes the child tumble into sadness and despair. This is a real event, regardless of what others say to the child. It is difficult to shake.

There is a tendency to ignore the problems of a Smart Kid. They were able to work through challenges and succeed in the past. They could "get over it and move on." They are not troublemakers. They are perceived as having it all together. Just look at their grades! All must be well. This is a false idea. Every child, regardless of intelligence, struggles with what they personally perceive as problems.

I hate my life.

I am here. Don't you see me?

I am not smart all the time.

Smart Kids may have a perception that they are being ignored and not seen as special by parents, teachers, or other authority figures because they behave and do what is expected. This is an emotionally intense perception that can gain traction in the teen years. This feeling of being misunderstood emotionally harms a child.

I don't want to be smart anymore.

Everyone is happy but me.

Don't you notice that there is a dark cloud in my world?

Teens often make critical judgments of themselves and others. This generates stress in comparing their abilities or non-abilities to peers. Even advanced intelligence will not help a child become a star baseball player. The child might be experiencing walls or barriers to their efforts, and it might be the first time they are not immediately excelling at an activity.

Parents may witness their child's heightened sensitivity to situations that are described as unfair or unjust. This lack of power to change a situation creates frustration and anger. Take these opportunities to talk about how the world's systems are not always fair to all people.

Depression can manifest in physical ailments such as stomachaches, no desire to eat, and acne. Disappearing is easy for the Smart Kid. They have the ability to self-isolate without generating a concern from parents. "I need to study." The door is closed, and their support system is blocked off.

Managing the blues

Stay alert to changes. Notice everything. This does not mean a verbal interpretation of the child's behavior or choices is necessary. Just observe, allow time for the child to make decisions or change their behavior on their own. This self-regulation is what is desired.

Be present. Parents have busy lives outside of raising children. This is good for the adults and the child. No teen wants or needs to be the constant focus of the adults in their life. However, a plethora of potential issues are avoided by being physically present and routinely spending time with a teen. This is not the time to "stop raising" children. They always need parental support.

This teen is changing. Understand that the Smart Kid's high intellectual complexity is now paired with an equally intense emotional depth. Teach resilience by keeping conversations open. Use examples of real-life scenarios of concern that illustrate success in positive decision making.

Let a child be a child. These are not small adults. The critical judgment of a parent has the power to destroy a child's self-efficacy. Use this power by changing judgment into encouragement. For example, allow the child to determine the rules and schedules in a household. The Smart Kid should be a part of the decision on determining consequences prior to any infractions.

Make good things happen. Parents have the ability to provide positive experiences for their family on a predictable basis. It is surprising how these events impact a child's wellbeing. The length of time of an event is not as important as the positive nature of a family gathering. Everyone participates. All conversations are positive. Laughter is essential.

Talk about it. Start the conversation by sitting with hands free of distractions (no phones, etc.). This is a simple technique. The child knows the parent is not leaving any time soon. Talk about non-confrontational subjects first. Listen, then listen some more. Lots of nodding and probing into what the child sees as important, not the parent. Ask for small details to keep the conversation going. This *"talking it out"* is often used to de-escalate a depressive state. Never insult a child's opinion or give an opinion too soon. This stops the conversation.

Is alone time good or bad? Remember a tendency for social isolation may just be a need to reset and rest. Know when to step in if a child is fiercely guarding their alone time. Parents need to have respectful access to a child's area.

Be alert, and ready to take action if observations find emotional and physical indications a child needs professional counseling. This counseling may start with a parent's conversation with a school counselor. Ask direct questions. Give examples of the child's words and behavior.

Know when to hire a mental health professional or get immediate help for a child. Most veteran teachers and administrators have experience with children who are clinically or mildly depressed. Risk assessments are conducted according to district protocols to determine the gravity of the risk. The child's safety is paramount. Parents are involved in every step and advised to seek the advice of a mental health professional when a child's safety is at risk.

"I am not good at anything anymore!"

A series of failures or non-perfect results can become a big deal to the Smart Kid. In many circumstances, the parental approach has the power to determine the outcome. Utilize unyielding patience and the knowledge of the child's motivators and fears to offer help. Know when to allow the child to fail and when to offer gentle guidance and assistance. When talking, highlight the positives first, then move toward suggested changes.

These psychological pains are felt deeply. The child's journey can be filled with angst, self-doubt, and internal turmoil. Most often the Smart Kid has always been at the top of their academic peer group. Defeat is felt severely because it is far outside their norm. The Smart Kid places additional pressure on themselves to continue their high level of success in school. These expectations for themselves and others are felt as a heavy burden when they are not succeeding. Pressures rise when Smart Kids notice their inability to keep up. They have never been lower than the top 1% of the class. They no longer fit into their social group.

The indicators of mental health difficulties are first seen by those closest to the child. Pay attention to friends, teachers, or siblings who can alert the parent to a negative change. Follow through with an investigation. Look for signs of bullying. Do not be put off by the child. This trauma can be hidden – gently dig for it.

Parents only know what their teens want them to know

Information about a child's life is a privilege, and it is up to the child whether they wish to share it. This is an exercise of independence and not a slight on the parent. Only by building trust, giving space, and staying alert will a parent learn negative or harmful information.

Listen to those parental instincts. Notice small changes in attitude and behavior. Stay close... but not too close. This is a tightrope. Ask questions. School staff are often the first to notice changes. Keep a positive and open dialogue with teachers, counselors, school nurses, etc.

Tips for parents to help manage Smart Kid stress

Create a predictable home environment. Keep up established and agreed upon routines.

Keep consistent expectations of each family member. Different ages may mean different tasks but not expectations.

Keep positive family routines including dinner, games, movie night, etc.

Stay on schedule for homework, bedtime, and meals.

Keep a calm environment by removing clutter or over-stimulating electronics.

Listen to concerns. Patiently interpret their own meanings.

Visually and verbally walk through a future potentially upsetting event. These clear steps provide predictability and avoid emotional surprises.

Adapted from *Smart Kid Terminology* (Small, 2022b)

Resources for further study

Allbright, T. N., Marsh, J. A., Kennedy, K. E., Hough, H. J., & McKibben, S. (2019). Social-emotional learning practices: Insights from outlier schools. *Journal of Research in Innovative Teaching and Learning, 12*(1), 35–52.

Course Hero. (2022). Time management. www.coursehero.com /file/93640748/5-type-of-study-skillspptx/

Craig, W. M., & Pepler, D. J. (2003). Identifying and targeting risk for involvement in bullying and victimization. *Canadian Journal of Psychiatry, 48*(9), 577–582.

Davidson Institute. (n.d.). Resources for gifted children & their families. www.davidsongifted.org

Davidson institute for talent development, helping your gifted child adjust to middle school, November 20, 2020. https//www.davidsongifted.org/gifted-blog/helping-your -gifted-child-adjust-to-midle-school/

Frog Pond Theory Resource: NOBA is the Diener Education Fund, a non-profit organization. https://nobaproject.com /modules/social-comparison, Visualization of the theory: www.youtube.com/watch?v=1p3X-iFCWqA.

Goodman, S. (2014). Fuel creativity in the classroom with divergent thinking. Edutopia. www.edutopia.org/blog /fueling-creativity-through-divergent-thinking-classroom -stacey-goodman

Hamachek, D. E. (1978). Psychodynamics of normal and neurotic perfectionism. *Psychology, 15*, 27–33.

Jung, J. Y., Jackson, R. L., Townend, G., & McGregor, M. (2022). Equity in gifted education: The importance of definitions and a focus on underachieving gifted students. *Gifted Child Quarterly, 66*(2), 149–151. https://doi.org/10.1177/00169862211037945

McCoach, D., & Siegle, D. (2005). Making a difference: Motivating gifted students who are not achieving. *Teaching Exceptional Children, 38*(1), 22–27.

Miedijensky, S. (2018). Learning environment for the gifted – What do outstanding teachers of the gifted think? *Gifted Education International, 34*(3), 222–244.

Multon, K. D., Brown, S. D., & Lent, R. W. (1991). Relation of self-efficacy beliefs to academic outcomes: A meta-analytic investigation. *Journal of Counseling Psychology, 38*(1), 30–38. http://doi.org/10.1037/0022-0167.38.1.30

National Association for Gifted Children. (2011). Redefining giftedness for a new century: Shifting the paradigm. www.nagc.org/uploadedFiles/About_NAGC/Redefining%20Giftedness%20for%20a%20New%20Century.pdf

National Association for Gifted Children. (n.d. a). Underachievement. www.nagc.org/resources-publications/resources/achievement-keeping-your-child-challenged/underachievement

National Association for Gifted Children. (n.d. b). Supporting twice-exceptional students. www.nagc.org/twice-exceptional-home-and-school

Perfectionist (n.d.). In Oxford English dictionary. https://www.oxfordreference.com/display/10.1093/oi/authority.20110803100317773;jsessionid=61277070EE869E5BB9489AADE0C2CCFA

PACE working paper, which can be found here. https://edpolicyinca.org/publications/gender-differences-students-self-efficacy

Peterson, J., Canady, K., & Duncan, N. (2012). Positive life experiences: A qualitative, cross-sectional, longitudinal study of gifted graduates. *Journal for the Education of the Gifted, 35*(I), 81–99.

Renzulli, J. S. (2009). *Operation houndstooth: A positive perspective on developing social intelligence.* Routledge

Van Tassel-Baska, J., Cross, T.L., & Olenchak, F.R. (Eds.). (2009). *Social-Emotional Curriculum With Gifted and Talented Students* (1st ed.). Routledge. https://doi.org/10.4324/9781003238065

Siegle, D. (2013). *The underachieving gifted child: Recognizing, understanding, and reversing underachievement.* Prufrock Press.

Small, B. K. (2022a). *Serving the needs of your smart kids: How school leaders create a supportive school culture for the advanced learner.* Gifted Unlimited, LLC.

Small, B. K. (2022b). *Smart kid terminology: 25 terms to help gifted learners see themselves and find success.* Routledge.

Van Tassel-Baska, J. L., Cross, T. L., & Olenchak, F. R. (Eds.). *Social-emotional curriculum with gifted and talented students* (pp. 79–112). Prufrock Press.

Wood, S. (2010). Best practices in counseling the gifted in schools: What's really happening? *Gifted Child Quarterly, 54*(1), 42–58. https://doi.org/10.1177/0016986209352681

Chapter 3

The Wisdom of School People

DOI: 10.4324/9781003332817-3

Chapter 3

Tip #11

I must think about this problem... odd... learning how to learn is not easy

Is *Learning Imprinting* possible? The definition of this is learning how to learn by watching and experiencing. Therefore, it may well be possible, but not always for the benefit of the Smart Kid. An infant starts their young life immersed in the learning process. This ability to learn stays with them as they grow into a toddler and then preschooler. Imprinting takes place during this time when the child learns at an accelerated pace. This quick mastery leads the child to believe this is how learning occurs. There are few challenging lessons.

Past learning experiences influence the future learning experiences of the advanced learner. A child who received easy A's in elementary school assumes future grade level work will follow this pattern. The young student simply listens to the teacher and produces the top product in the class. These high-achieving students quickly learn to discern what is needed to receive the top grade. It may not be their best work, but it satisfies the teacher and parents.

This method of minimal learning may seem like a reward for the high-level learner's intellectual abilities. However, the child's mindset must drastically change when they enter a school or class with content at or above their learning level. This placement into a properly challenging learning environment opens up an alternative perspective of their own abilities.

Parent: My child has always been very bright. Your school is not teaching him correctly. He says others are getting higher grades. I need you to give him accommodations so he will continue to recieve high grades.

Student: This teacher does not know what she is doing. We have to do all the work. She never answers my questions. She makes me find the answers.

This makes me tired and frustrated.

Teacher: Studying is not the same as learning. He needs different study tools to learn material. I will help with some suggestions.

Parent: My student studies all the time. I see him reading and working on that subject every night. Why does he earn such low-test grades when he studies all the time?

Parent: My child received a B on a test. This has never happened before.

What is wrong with that teacher?

Doesn't she know how to grade?

Learning How to Learn breaks down previous study habits

The early *Learning Imprinting* is replaced at the secondary level with the struggle of *Learning How to Learn*. This process is watched and evaluated by parents. There are moans, groans, poor grades, defeatist attitudes, blaming, and hours spent staring at textbook pages. These are new behaviors for their child. Parents take their concerns to the teacher and the principal's office with a worried need to discover why there is a change in their child's behavior and environment.

The child who successfully learns to process challenging information will build a collection of problem-solving skills. These newly learned skills can be applied to future challenges. This is a critical skill in *Learning How to Learn*.

Well-trained teachers in gifted education build lessons with embedded challenges that students may not be able to master with previous skills. If a student is not familiar with the feeling of being challenged, these strategies are perceived as barriers or walls to "get around." Keen teachers make sure there is no potential for "getting around" the challenge.

Parents witness the child encountering such barriers with patience and curiosity. They see how the results create a new appreciation for learning in their child. This rigor is a "runner's high" to a Smart Kid. The solution to a problem is discovered through the flexing of intellectual muscles and often collaboration with like-minded young scholars.

Below are some examples of what may occur in the home of the Smart Kid between them and their parents when *Learning How to Learn* starts to occur.

> *Scenario*: Observe the studious child. Sitting in their study area looking interested in their homework assignment. The click of the keyboard with a periodic hum of the printer. Of course, she is studying!
>
> *Look closer.* She has earbuds in for her clandestine concert, podcast, or novel.
>
> She is aware of where the authority figure is in the house and that they are listening to her movements and sounds. It is not difficult for a child of any age to provide the expected sounds.

Enter the parent. "How is studying going? Do you like the assigned book? Do you have a test tomorrow?" *Student*: "Good, it's OK, no."

Try this instead: *Enter the parent.* "What are you learning? Teach it to me."

Student: "Why, you don't have to know this stuff? Fine, we are learning about Shakespeare's *Romeo and Juliet*. We are in Act II. They are..."

Student: "This class is more difficult than classes last year. The teacher does not give clear explanations. She says it is a 'holistic' way of teaching and learning. We are supposed to 'learn by doing.' Figure it out on our own. Well, I have a D in this class because I can't figure it out."

Teacher: "Tell me what you are trying to figure out in your own words. Be specific. Now, think about what is needed to get to that point. Ok, which needs to be completed first, second, and third? Why is this important for the final outcome? Good, let's get started."

Holistic learning is common in the classroom of high-level learners who have knowledgeable and well-trained teachers. This is only one example of a type of learning in such a classroom.

Step 1: Recognize the type of learning. There are three types of holistic learning: experiential, self-guided, and independent learning.

Step 2: Slow down. Look at the assignment. Many times, holistic learning starts with only a description of the final result.

Step 3: Begin with the end in mind. Listen to peers. Their "giftedness" may be different which makes collaboration an extraordinary experience. Learn from peers as they learn from you.

This is common sense. Yes, but there is nothing *common* about *sense* when emotions are involved in changing a lifelong pattern of learning practices. The feeling of not being the smartest in a class is odd and threatening to some children. Equally as jarring to their self-image is the inability to figure something out quickly with the familiar tools that have worked in the past.

Here are five starter suggestions for *Learning to Learn* and not just studying

1. *Lists and calendars are a child's friend.* Time management becomes more concrete when it is incorporated into a list. Add dates and times by the items on the list. Even better, include the use of a printed-out calendar. The calendar and the lists make the completing of the items on the list fun to cross out.

2. *Organization is important to the learner.* Poor organization is like a dangerous beast in a child's mind. "Where is this? What was I supposed to do with this page? When is this due? Why did everyone else turn in an assignment today?" Release the beast from the child's mind by creating a space for organization and routines.

3. *When will motivation arrive?* This is an important concept for both adults and children. Know when the mind is ready for input and output. Early in the morning is not a good time for adolescents. But younger children thrive in the morning. Completing schoolwork immediately after school may not work for all children. They need "down time" to take a mind break. They may have greater motivation to produce a better result closer to or after dinner time.

4. *Chunking is where it's at.* Imagine the list of homework to be completed for one night. There is English, Science, Technology, and, of course, math. It is human nature to complete homework from a favorite class first. Yes, creating a schematic for Technology to use on the robots tomorrow is exactly how the student wants to spend their time. But wait, after their favorite homework is completed and then the next favorite, there is an exhaustion factor. The student's class with the lowest grade is probably also their least favorite. Chunk this subject first. Take it on with high motivation to complete it and move on to the homework for their

favorite class. Take breaks and maybe even change the study location for different subjects.

5. *Write it down = Note taking.* Many Smart Kids have a keen ability to listen to the teacher and be successful in completing a test or assignment without writing one word of an explanation or lecture. As subjects become more difficult to master, note taking becomes critical. A student cannot jump into effective note taking without practice. By starting with easier classes, the note taking muscles start to develop. There is a phenomenon which occurs in a student's notes. Their abbreviations, organization through outlines, entire sentences, column symbols, and so on take shape. These will be the same techniques used in college to study Business, Law, Medicine, etc. The sharpening of these skills starts in kindergarten through to 12th grade.

Remember, children are not their parent's *Mini-Me's.* They have their own physiological characteristics and intellectual personalities that are different from a parent or other authority figure. This is the reason patience and support are critical pillars in the creation of environments that are safe and fun to *Learn How to Learn.*

Hack

So, you have been taking easy subjects so you can get perfect grades. The ramifications of these choices come to roost when a new subject is attempted.

Study like a university student:

1. If you can teach it, you know it.
2. Read once, then rewrite the key points on sticky notes; highlight one word at a time - use these prompts to explain what is in the paragraph in your own words.
3. Make diagrams and charts to organize the content.
4. Color-code with the themes in the study material.
5. Make a tangible and manipulatable object with the content.
6. Read out loud while acting the part of the teacher.

Tip #12

You want my Smart Kid in Classes for the Gifted? But they aren't one of "those" kids

What to do? Does a parent listen to the gossip about Smart Kid classes?

How can a parent differentiate between what is true and what is not true about these special classes?

These are common thoughts in parents of students who have recently been identified as gifted. A family may have changed schools and their gifted child is placed in *Classes for the Gifted* for the first time. Or a parent may have decided it is time to take advantage of the acceleration opportunities in a school.

There are several times in a student's kindergarten through 12th grade school experience that their *giftedness* may be discovered. Students are generally screened in the 2nd or 3rd grade. Once identified, the child can receive services from their teacher, school, or district.

Universal screening has become common national practice. "Universal" means that *all* students are screened at a predetermined grade level. The students usually do not need a referral from a parent or teacher to start the process. This later screening commonly occurs in 6th grade. The rationale for this is that, first, 10- to 12-year-old adolescents have arrived in their middle school from a variety of elementary schools that may or may not have screening in early grades. Second, students may experience a higher intellectual acuity at this stage and be successfully screened into the gifted program.

What are the choices for a gifted student's placement?

The answer depends on how the teacher, school, and district meet the state and national requirements to serve a student identified as gifted. Find the choices on the school's or district's website. A call to the Gifted and Talented Resource Office is often required to answer questions about options. Within each of the options below are academic strategies for acceleration.

The National Association for Gifted Children lists the common options as:

✓ Students remain in their regular classroom with added accommodations.

✓ Part-time placement in one or two advanced learning classes.

✓ Students attend classes with others of similar abilities.

✓ Students are moved to a higher grade level.

Why should my child receive accommodations or be placed in "Classes for the Gifted?"

There is a tribe out there with each member having the same unique characteristics of being a gifted human. At each age level, these members think differently than others of the same age that are outside their tribe.

Their high intellect makes them see the world through a lens not understood by their average peers. The social support of this tribe is obvious. When they are together, their words come easily and are understood. Their desires to explore, experience, and understand drive friendships. More importantly, they do not feel different when they are together. This is important because a culture may define "different" as wrong or abnormal. The parent will notice this tribe even though they may be the outsider.

Academically, the high-level learner often has a choice to be with students equal to or above their own intelligence. They may seek such like-minded intellectuals who challenge their thinking and help them grow. Their teachers can present challenges that are tackled in groups of forward and "out-of-the-box" thinkers. These peers may be from mixed grades and include asynchronously gifted children of varying high levels of academic ability.

Choosing not to be in "Classes for the Gifted"

In contrast, a child may prefer to remain the smartest student in their class or group. Their desire is to keep acceleration to a minimum. But why? There are several emotional, social, and intellectual reasons. These regular groups keep the Smart Kid's academic position as *special* and at the top of the class. Less challenge translates into less effort. And what child doesn't want to feel special with very little effort?

Placing a student with high intelligence into a class with average learners may be the child's choice. A reputation as being "one of *those* Smart Kids" may drive the decision to stay among average peers. Advanced classes are filled with Smart Kids who may seem different, perhaps nerd-like. Plus, these Smart Kids know all the answers and are not afraid to let everyone in the class know that they are smart. The expectation to have similar motivations in such an academically driven environment creates pressure and stress.

Other parents will express their opinion on what choices are best. They may try to persuade others to stay away from, or stay in, accelerated classes due to their own child's experience. Do not fall for this. Every child is different. "Parent recruiters" may not have the best interests of your child in mind.

A school's culture may be set up to praise sports or clubs and not intellectual acuity. This is difficult to combat when peers are popular for abilities outside of their schoolwork. Frequently, coveted electives are not available for the Smart Kids. These may be technical, non-academic, and career-oriented classes. Students in these specialized programs become their own cohort of friends. A Smart Kid may not want to give up this tribe to attend accelerated classes with intellectual equals.

What to do?

These internal dialogues will drive the decision on placement into gifted or regular courses. Listen and learn from the child's descriptions of their school world. Family talk is essential before making any move. These are choices which will impact the child's education and future.

If a teen is newly identified as gifted or is considering accepting accommodations, there is work to do. These budding young adults have preconceived ideas about such programs, grown out of their personal experiences. They are filled with self-doubt even though outwardly confident. Talk about giftedness often and with honesty. This helps to normalize their feelings and their situation. Keep conversations light and always end on a positive note.

Younger children will seek definitions that describe themselves. Provide details about the assessments to determine giftedness. Go through the traits of gifted children. Ask their opinions on their own identified traits. Discuss how these characteristics may impact their relationships with both adults and other children. Explain that everyone learns at a different pace and students identified as gifted still need to study and will sometimes struggle to learn. Seek to relieve the anxiety of high expectations.

The act of "gifted shaming" must be avoided. A parent may internally question why their child can solve a complex math problem but cannot find their shoes. Or how their child's can remember a geographical location they visited when they were 3 years old yet does not bring home the correct textbooks. Parents should use supportive language and suggest tools for success.

There should be no threats to remove a child from high academic classes because they earned a low grade. These are children with ebbs and flows of attention coupled with inconsistent application of their intelligence. Ride the wave to adulthood with them by making their experiences positive and nurturing their intelligence.

Next steps

Remember, the parent is in control. Yes, education acronyms, systems, and schedules are frequently intimidating to a parent. But hold strong and ask questions until the answers are given. The parent has the final choice on placement and accommodations. Working diligently to understand the needs of a gifted child will lead the parent to make the best decisions for their child.

Decisions are never permanent. School policies, staff, and options change just as quickly as the child changes. A decision made one year for a 4th grader may not be the same decision made for the same child when they are a 5th grader. Students and their parents both grow in their knowledge and requirements over time. Stay on top of any changes.

Tip #13

Too cool for school!

Student: I just want to learn something new! None of the kids know as much as me. This is not how I learn.

Parent: My child never seems to encounter a situation where self-discipline and study skills are needed.

Student: I am smarter than the teacher, again, this year. I am finished with this school! Why go when I am not learning anything?

Irritation and frustration can be seen in a Smart Kid's inability to change their current educational situation. They sound off about how others are not as smart as them, including their teachers.

Subjects are repeated between grade levels. Curriculum is even repeated. The Smart Kid has a brilliant memory and does not understand why they have to cover the subject again. *Let's move on to something new and interesting.*

The teachers know the child knows the answer. They eventually refrain from calling on the Smart Kid. Teachers are accommodating with frequent praise as they recognize they know the answer… every time. They want other students to engage in the conversation. Sometimes their peers answer incorrectly. This causes more frustration for the Smart Kid.

"I told my teacher I could explain these math problems to the class better than her." The social ramifications of answering out or always knowing the answer add to the

angst. Perfect grades and a superior academic demeanor only add to the Smart Kid's feeling of being different. The other students treat them different… because they are different. They have not found "their people" or "tribe" yet. The school may not group students by ability (honors, AP, gifted, etc.) but by age or grade level.

The textbooks or other class materials also add to the frustration. Much of the information can be outdated or rudimentary. The knowledgeable and interested young scholar is aware of more current or more advanced information. A correction of the teacher or contribution of evidence is not always appreciated by authority. Nonetheless, students often feel it is their obligation to let the teacher or parent know when they are wrong.

A student who feels "too cool for school" has a tendency to have a wandering mind during classes. They will quickly point out that this does not matter. The teacher keeps repeating the same message and content. They only have to "half listen" to keep up with the class. Smart Kids may shift their mind to a favorite subject as a distraction in class and fail the current in-class assignment.

These are all symptoms of Smart Kid burnout, due to improper class or school placement. The feelings that accompany this "too cool for school" attitude are not to be dismissed. They demand attention. Parents have the power to seek answers from teachers and the leaders of the school.

Suggestions for school communication:

1. Ask the teacher, counselor, administrator: Why does my child feel this way in these classes?
2. Give specific examples of repeating materials between grade levels.
3. Ask for the acceleration policy of the school and district. Written policies are required by most states.
4. Ask what the options are in terms of pull-out or placement into a higher-level class. Do not be satisfied with the answer that students are only grouped by age/grade level. Fight for a proper academic placement.
5. Meet with the teacher assigned to the Gifted and Talented program or a teacher who has the highest ability students in the school. Ask for ideas and materials to use in the home to accelerate the child's learning.

Working toward creating a more accelerated learning environment

Listen to the student's frustrations. Work with them to implement socially acceptable solutions in a classroom. There are alternative responses or actions to take when they know the answer in class. Also, seek accelerated placement into an honors level, gifted, higher grade, advanced placement, or other accelerated option. Don't give up. Keep asking the school to make accommodations.

Knowledgeable teachers will adapt individual learning and allow the student to be "off task" and read on their own during lectures. Their grades will reveal if this strategy is working. These teachers provide different and accelerated assignments, not additional classwork.

Classes structured to meet the needs of high-level learners often work in groups. This collaboration to solve problems together gives opportunities to share what students already know and how to find new knowledge together. Advanced placement and honors teachers know how to meet the needs of their Smart Kids. Listen to what these teachers say about the learning environment.

Parents know their child and realize their understanding is increasing at an accelerated rate. Encourage the child to communicate about their experiences in class and at home. "I want to know it all" does not make me a "know it all." They thrive on rigor. Supplement the subjects of interest. Take it to the next level. Work within their unique skill set to encourage a deeper understanding through experiences outside of the classroom.

Bored at school

A bored student is not a happy student. There is a danger of disengagement from school. There are many subjects and activities out there that are less than healthy for a bored young mind. Keep an eye on behaviors and keep communication open.

Too many lessons are not differentiated for students who are wired for complexity and need the rigor. These mass lessons are a waste of their time. Compliance with sitting in a classroom will only last so long before the Smart Kid bolts or shuts down. It is easy to stay "off the radar" in a classroom.

Managing boredom starts with open conversations with the child. Find out which teachers use accelerated classroom techniques such as flexible grouping, collaboration, and self-paced learning experiences. Use parent power to strategically place the child in the correct learning environment.

The home should be a safe place to express frustration and boredom. Do not shut this down. Listen with interest and offer encouragement and solutions. The predictability of constant support keeps a Smart Kid emotionally strong.

Most school topics are easy to accelerate with a creative deep dive into the subject. This could be a science experiment, a museum trip, or a building project. Include friends from the class. Get the parents together to talk about how to extend the learning for the group.

The needs of the accelerated learner will bubble up. A statement that they are bored in school is a sign that there are needs that must be addressed. These social and emotional needs are expressed in different ways that require an aware parent to notice. Parents are on the front line in helping their Smart Kid navigate their options by providing support, acknowledgement, and taking action.

HACK

"I am going to call your teacher and find out the truth!"

It is time to reach out to your child's teacher. Here are the do's and don'ts:

- ✓ Do be brief and to the point.
- ✓ Don't try to be friends, there is not time for this.
- ✓ Do take the time to talk and give your full attention, especially if the teacher calls you.
- ✓ Take notes with dates, times, and future plans.
- ✓ Don't assume your child tells the truth.
- ✓ Do not interrupt, do share your ideas.
- ✓ Do not look for a quick fix, change takes time.
- ✓ Don't get defensive.
- ✓ Your child may have one personality at home and another at school.

Tip #14

Help! School conferences never end how I want them to end… ever!

Why parent–teacher conferences go south

A parent observes their child's grades and behavior at home. They listen to the child's excuses of why they are not meeting expectations. Situations vary as much as the number of children in the school.

Let's get to the bottom of this. It is time to meet with the teachers and find out why this child is not thriving.

This is the typical set up for the parent–teacher conference:

Scenario #1:

The parent contacts the school counselor and requests a conference with all the child's teachers. Within a week or two, the meeting is set. (Elementary conferences will include fewer staff members. Secondary conferences should include all teachers and other staff. For example, the Gifted and Talented teacher, all subject teachers, the school counselor, and the parent.) The counselor meets the parent in the front office. The student is called to the office. They are placed in a room (conference room or classroom) to await the teachers.

The conference starts with a presentation of the grades by the counselor or lead teacher. The student listens silently. The Gifted and Talented teacher reviews the required accommodations. Each teacher reports on the reason for the student's status and performance in their class. The child sits with her chin on her chest, watching the clock. All leave with an "action plan" made by the adults. Will anything change and make a difference in the life of the child?

There is little doubt that conferences like these will be unsuccessful. This is a *system-oriented* conference model. More specifically, this is an *adult-oriented* conference model. The child is the receiver of information. Their input on their performance is less important than the input of the adults.

Consider the gifted child who has been navigating their primary or secondary education daily for many years. They watch and experience the various acceleration options, from getting pulled out of classes, to being assigned more difficult work and even spending down time grading the papers of other students.

This type of conference is their only experience with their counselor and teachers. If they have chosen to let a few subjects slide, they will be familiar with the rhetoric. "Try harder. You are smarter than this." This Smart Kid can predict what will happen in the room prior to the arrival of the adults.

One high-level learner related this honest opinion of a parent–teacher conference:

> *"They go around the table and talk about me. Then, they come up with a plan for me to do things differently. Everyone leaves the room with smirking faces. Mom is angrier than when it started. She seems*

a little confused. Then we have new rules at home for about a month. I guess, it takes me about that long to decide whether to do what they want me to do or if they give up. It's not too difficult to keep off their radar."

Consider this unique model built for the high-level learner

Review the objective of the conference as a meeting to determine why a student is underperforming (do note there are a plethora of other reasons to call a conference too: this objective is used as an example to illustrate the model). If the child is the focus of the conference, why are they not speaking on their own behalf?

The following is instead the set up for a "student–parent conference":

Scenario #2:

The parent asks for a conference through the school's communication system and arrives 15 minutes prior to the appointment time. Their 10th grader is retrieved from class to meet in the conference center. He meets mom in the reception area. Both are escorted to the small conference room or classroom.

The school counselor enters with a greeting to both. She gives the student a sheet of paper. This is the agenda for the conference. She explains how the student is leading the conference. The parent is puzzled but intrigued.

The four teachers arrive and sit at the circular table. The student sits in the designated leader seat with the counselor and parent close but not next to him. He begins with an "opening statement" as directed by the agenda.

"Hi, thank you for being here. This should only take 30 minutes. Each of you has a copy of my grades in front of you. We will all have input on my progress. (This may be a pre-written introduction that he reads or a generic one written by the counselor.) First, my statement:

I have been absent many days this term because I have a hard time getting up for the 6:30am bus. Mom works the night shift and gets home after I leave. John, my little brother, gets up better than I do. We walk to the bus stop together. I try to get my homework done. Sometimes I don't see the point. It's just busy work. I ace the tests but all of you mark me down for homework. Now to my teachers: Ms. Jackson, Mom, she is my Algebra 2 teacher. I have a 62% in your class (looking at Ms. Jackson) because of homework. The tests are only worth 50% of the grade."

Ms. Jackson reports on how the proportional value of the tests and homework is decided. Homework helps with work ethic… the conference continues until all teachers have reported and the parent and counselor respond with clarifying questions.

The conference concludes 5 minutes prior to the ending time. The student wraps up the teacher comments and writes down (or it is written for him by the counselor) the two to three solutions offered. He may be prompted by the adults but makes his own decision on what is written.

Notice the attention is on the child who knows why they are earning their current grades. This is not new information to the child. If the environment of this student–parent conference is set up as a safe and blame-free zone, the adults will learn more about the child. Isn't that the point of the conference?

The counselor's agenda and the reports from the teachers do not drive the conference. Yes, their opinions are important. But a focus on what the child says is the most important part of the conference. Students with high intelligence may either like or hate this type of conference. But they must participate. They are the star performer.

If all conferences in the child's school are conducted in this manner, the student will be able to predict what will take place in the next student–parent conference. This could help to dissuade them from allowing their grades to fall. The student knows they cannot simply sit and say, "I will try harder." Their detailed explanations and opinions are the focus of the next conference.

The parent's role in the student–parent conference

Prepare:

1. Keep a file at home with a copy of the past agreements for accommodations and communications from teachers indicating the meeting of such accommodations. Bring the file to the conference. Keep it closed and ready if needed.

2. Print out the child's grades from the student management system. Usually this is online and updated by the teacher when completed assignments are entered.

3. Write a list of questions and concerns. Listen for the answers which may come up without having to ask questions. Keep questions concise and to the point. This is the student's time, not a time for the parent to pontificate about their own school experiences or the details of their home experiences.

During the student–parent conference:

1. The student will lead the conference. Period. No one should interrupt them. The counselor or lead teacher will follow the agenda, keep time, and prompt the student.

2. Be patient. The child may be using new skills. Their leadership may be slow and awkward. This is because the adults are not leading the conference. It is worth the wait to nurture the student. Remember the objective of the conference.

3. Interrupt and advocate for the child if the adults are disrespectful or interrupt the student with corrections. They will get their chance to speak.

4. When the teachers report, ask specific questions about the grading percentages: homework, tests, classwork, etc. Be confident in bringing attention to specific assignments.

5. Listen to the teachers. Listen for key words that describe the student in ways the parent has not noticed. The teacher's observations may be important in determining the social, emotional, or academic reasons a child is struggling. A warning about the student-led conference is the student's ability to avoid bringing up uncomfortable topics.

6. Parents should refrain from:

    - Asking for a daily email update on progress.
    - Asking for more communication from the teacher than once a week.
    - Demanding to see graded work.
    - Telling the teachers that they are the issue, not the student.
    - Telling the teachers that the child studies every night for hours. Why are they failing the assignments? The answer is simple: because "studying" and "learning" are different. The Smart Kid may be fooling you. Any gifted child knows how to pretend to be studying when a parent is nearby. Ask the child to teach you the topic. They cannot fake that!

Successful student–parent conferences meet these objectives

1. The student leaves the conference feeling empowered to make sustainable changes.

2. The teachers and counselor leave the conference knowing their opinions and suggestions have been valued.

3. The negotiated solutions were determined by the student. Each adult present had a voice in the action plan, but the final crafting of the solutions was by the student.

4. Parents leave the conference having new information solicited by their child during the conference.

5. Parents leave the conference knowing their opinions were considered and their child was the most important person in the room. Everyone came to an understanding even if they all had different opinions.

6. All leave the conference with a commitment to the solutions proposed by the student.

A few words about school counselors

Parents may ask "Who is the school counselor and what can they do for me?" The role of a school counselor has changed in the past decade. These masters-degree professionals bring quality education and experiences to our students and school staff.

School counselors are often the child's advocate and a "soft place to land" in a school. Yet, their responsibilities and accountability have increased substantially. Consequently, their priorities often shift to the lower-level learners and students struggling to be promoted to the next grade or even to graduate. Keep in mind, most counselors selected this profession to serve the students, not necessarily the parents of students.

High-level learners and their parents will be most successful when a positive relationship is built with the school counselor. By acknowledging the counselor is overworked, the parent can come up with a savvy plan to gain their attention and the information they need. Start with knowing the time of the school year or the time of day that the counselor is relaxed and available for discussions. Bringing a positive and knowledgeable presence is the best start to this relationship.

What is the typical role of the school counselor in a school?

Yes! School Counselors are	**Nope! School Counselors are not**
the heart of a school	mental health counselors
a soft place to land for children	experts on subjects taught

a great resource to talk about universities and careers	information sources about other students, parents, administrators, or schools
able to change a student's teacher or class schedule if they want to...☺	experts on gifted education policies and procedures
prone to work harder for positive people than mean people (whether a teacher, parent, student, or administrator)	secretaries for the administration or teaching staff
extremely busy during the opening and closing weeks of school	knowledgeable about the needs of every child
part of the child advocate team	looking at every child's grades every day

A school counselor may or may not have knowledge of high-level learners and gifted policies and procedures. Most will advise students and their families about acceleration options on and off campus. Parents of newly identified gifted children in elementary school will find their knowledgeable counselor an invaluable resource. Together with the counselor, the assigned Gifted and Talented teacher, and the classroom teachers, the child will receive the best service possible to accelerate their learning levels.

HACK

"Here I go, back to the school to meet with teachers."

1. Before arriving at a scheduled conference, send a list of expectations to the person leading the meeting. For example: I would like a grade report with comments from each of my child's teachers.
2. I would like all the teachers present.
3. I want my child to lead the conference by asking each teacher their interpretation of progress or lack of progress which may include discipline issues.
4. I want to leave with an action plan in writing developed by the committee.
5. I do not want the meeting to go over 45 minutes.
6. Take charge!

Tip #15

Parent power! Use it when you dare!

The power is here, and the parent has it!

It may not have been needed until the teenage years. This *power* has been resting and waiting to be accessed like a dormant volcano. Compliance works between a parent and their Smart Kid when all is well with grades, attitude, friends, home, etc. It may be obvious when this isn't the case, and your little stranger (who may be taller than you by now) silently enters the home. Or their appearance may be with a *Pow* and a *Bang* that shakes the house.

Parents watch as their child grows and changes physically, emotionally, and intellectually. They see the awkwardness appear and disappear as their young scholar adapts to their environment. The teen years demand a different set of rules and expectations. The advice in this section is the end result of decades of working with developing Smart Kids and their worried parents. All advocates want the child to succeed to the best of their learning abilities.

Smart Kids know their parent's hot buttons

Parent behaviors are predictable. Their anger in the past matches their anger in the future. A child has the ability to cause an issue or say a word that results in a predictable parental response. This manipulation is common. A parent who is feeling guilty about their decision to move the family, divorce, take drugs, etc. is an open invitation for an observant child to use these parental emotions for their own gain.

The parent has the power to combat this maneuvering by maintaining a non-emotional front with consistent expectations. Call it out when it occurs. Notify the child that their actions are obvious, and this manipulation will not work.

Parents discipline their children: It happens

"Here are the rules and if they are broken this is what happens." This is an effective practice that clarifies the consequences of unwanted behavior. The child may take the risk and break the rules. The punishment is the consequence for an objective defiance, better known as *"you knew this was wrong and you still did it."* The foresight demanded for this type of discipline is not difficult. Most parents know what behaviors are coming and set up the expectations with the consequence before they occur. Consistency and follow-through are critical.

Poor grades rarely improve with punishment. A child has control of their learning. Taking away possessions is often a welcome challenge and ineffective at changing unwanted behavior. Parents may note that even if the only thing left in a child's room is a mattress… their behavior remains unchanged. That is a "win" for the child. Incentivizing learning takes a more in-depth understanding of the problem. Remember, a parent's anger may be the reason for the child's behavior.

Every child has a currency

Finding the child's currency is the first step to changing behavior.

Incentives that match the child's currency change behavior. The Smart Kid will do what they want to do when they want to do it. Therefore appealing to their "wants" can move mountains. Family and friends can be included in the reward system. Pull together the tribe. Pressure from others such as peers, siblings, and grandparents can push forward change.

Possible currencies of the Smart Kid:

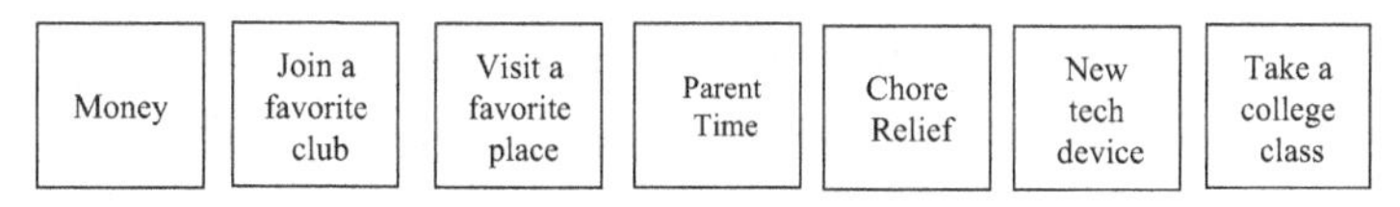

Give choices... but not too many

Direct orders often cause an emotional reaction when a child is maturing into adolescence. Choices are a simple technique to make everyone feel valued. For example, a younger child may be given a choice between the red or blue shoes. The parent slyly makes sure other inappropriate shoes are not one of the options. A choice is made, and the child feels empowered.

So, give a Smart Kid a choice of several options instead of telling them what to do. For example, give them the list of required school supplies and a budgeted dollar amount. Send them into the store to make the choices on their own.

Parents are present to guide, not to control the choices made. Yes, this will take twice as long, but the child will be empowered and must live with their selections.

Teens make choices without their parent's knowledge. They are aware of what the parent wants them to do. Do they do it? Or do they go against what is perceived as their parent's choice. By allowing the child to exercise their own control under parental supervision, these unhealthy choices are more likely to be avoided.

Give control every time it is safe and appropriate. Monitor, watch, listen, and be present to help the child through a less-than-desirable choice. These are life lessons. The choices get more intense as the child matures, but the technique continues to work. *"You may attend the University of Texas or Yale, but not Northwestern University."*

I am going down to that school!

A parent who advocates for their family is a powerful person. A positive school environment welcomes a parent with respect and concern each time they enter the school or when they communicate through email or telephone. An effective school leader ensures their school staff is trained with the expectation to serve parents quickly and professionally.

Parents believe their child is the most important person in the school. They are part of the education team advocating for their child. This should be clear to teachers, front office personnel, coaches, and school leadership. Serve parents as a member of the team.

School systems can stall a parent's communication about the needs of their child. A few short tips can help to break down barriers that stand in the way. Follow the suggestions below for positive interactions which lead to more positive outcomes and less frustration:

1. Appointments are critical.
    a. Alert a favored secretary that an appointment is needed. Give a time window in which the appointment is needed: "in the next two days, before Friday, today."
    b. Mention one or two short items to be discussed. This gives the administrator time to pull the student's record or find answers prior to the meeting. This is an efficient use of everyone's time. No one likes surprises.
    c. Remember that school personnel spend much of their workday "putting out fires" that are part of their reactionary daily routine. Therefore, appointments should usually be set early in the day or after the students leave campus in the afternoon.
    d. No appointments are made during lunch periods or dismissal. The safety of the student population is a priority.

2. Know who is in charge. It is not always the principal...

   a. Start with the staff member who has the ability to solve the problem at the grass roots level. For example, a parent who has an issue with their child's schedule will have a more productive meeting with the person who changes schedules. The counselor is usually the first point of contact.

   b. If the first meeting does not end with the desired outcome, go up the ladder of authority. In larger schools it is often the assistant principal who oversees school counselors. In smaller schools it is most likely the principal.

   c. If the issue is about a student discipline decision made by a dean or assistant principal, it is necessary to go to the top decision maker to express concern about what occurred. This is usually the principal or the head of school.

   d. Follow the ladder of authority until the issue is resolved. This may require going outside the school to the district office.

3. Do not take a NO from someone who cannot give a YES.

   a. School staff members do not have authority outside of their assignment.

b. Make sure the conversation is with a person who can meet the parent's request.

c. Have an open dialogue with the principal and hold administrators accountable.

4. Know and articulate the desired outcome.

a. Be able to say the same desired outcome in about three different ways. Start the conversation with "I need ____ / I want ____ / make a change to _____."

b. For example, "I believe the five-day suspension is too long." "It is best to shorten the suspension to two days." "Consideration of changing the suspension to two days would be appreciated." Interestingly, this method of communication during the meeting is highly effective.

c. Know how much you are willing to bend prior to the meeting. "OK, I will accept a three-day suspension."

5. Know your rights.

a. Is it legal? The school must follow the law of the district and the state. There is very little wiggle room with some school-based decisions.

b. Is your request different than current school policy? If so, ask them to change the policy. These are situations where parent requests are often met. For example, a child needs acceleration into a higher mathematics course. The school has not previously accommodated high-level learners by allowing them to mix with older students in higher-level courses. Ask for this accommodation and keep asking until it is granted. The "why" is obvious. The "how" is up to the school to change policy to meet the needs of an individual child. *Schools are run for the children, not the adults.*

6. Gather the troops.

   a. Talk to other parents. Ask open-ended questions about the issue to other parents of Smart Kids. Conversations with parents of older children help newer parents in a school navigate the complex systems (Small, 2022b).

   b. The parent-group conversations are most effective when their contents are known by the administration. Informally, let the school leaders know what is being said. A savvy principal listens and makes changes to meet the needs of the children prior to meeting with the parents.

   c. Find out how the issue was resolved in the past with other families. If this solution is acceptable, ask for it specifically. Each parent's child should have the same consideration as any past child.

   d. Parents are a powerful cohesive group who will come forward as needed. If this is not the parent's natural personality, simply be present… at ball games, assemblies, fundraisers, car lines, etc. Chat up the school leadership. Do this with the counselor, assistant principal, lead teacher, or principal. Make sure they know your name and your child's name. This will pay off in the future.

Tip #16

My Smart Kid wants to be homeschooled… Why would I do that? What about school choice?

Every school-aged Smart Kid has an opinion on how they are being schooled. For most children, this analysis of their school day is heartfelt and accurate. A student can and will thrive in the school environment. The school years will pass, and the child will eventually graduate. So, why homeschool?

The value of homeschool can be obvious if the conditions are right. The child's learning is the focus, not a school's systems or the learning of other children. The homeschool environment has the capacity to nurture the child at their current level of learning and understanding. Acceleration is based not on age, but on ability. There is no need to provide acceleration accommodations to one child while the other students enjoy a less rigorous assignment. The lens for achievement is solely on the child.

Three scenarios of homeschool conversations

Scenario 1: Wrong placement in school.

"I am so different from everyone in school. Will you homeschool me?

These classes are so easy. Everyone makes fun of me, so I don't even answer the teacher's questions anymore. That's why they don't like me. I know you have gone to the school to check if I can change classes. This class is not working. My teacher says I need to be in Ms. McDonald's class. Bucky is in that class, and he is like me. Can I go there tomorrow?"

Scenario 2: It may be time to select a different school.

"I am so different from everyone in school. Will you homeschool me?

This school doesn't have kids like me. They don't even have a robotics club like the school Joshua and Patty go to. I know it is not the school my sister went to, but she is like these people. Can I go to that other school? They have advanced classes and crazy-fun field trips, like they are going to the dinosaur park next week. I know it's farther away, but they have afterschool chess. You know I love chess. Let's carpool with Joshua's mom. Will you at least talk to his mom?"

Scenario 3: Why we like homeschool.

"I am so different from everyone in school. Will you homeschool me?

It happened again. They told me I can't go to my special class because the teacher is busy with another class. Now, I have to stay in my regular class. Mom, I learned that math three years ago. My teacher asked me to run errands for her after I grade papers. Why can't you homeschool me? I promise I won't be a problem. No one talks to me at my school. I know I can still take Mr. Patterson's engineering class. There are two homeschoolers in my class now."

A family's decision to homeschool

When the request for homeschool enters the family conversation, a parent's first action should be to get to the origin of the request. Why is the child requesting this form of schooling? Has something happened at school? Is the catalyst for the request a legitimate concern? Is the child placed in the correct class for their ability? What are the other acceleration options in the school? Did the child have a conversation with a homeschooled student? The parent will listen and evaluate the child's answer to these questions to determine the reason for the request.

It seems appealing to stay at home, sleep in, enjoy lunch with mom and play on the computer all day. But this is not an accurate description of homeschooling. Provide a reality check on this assumption by explaining the daily routine of a homeschooler.

Equally important is a conversation about potential bullying. Is the request to be homeschooled a result of pressure from other children? The school leaders and teachers need to be involved if this concern becomes a reality.

There are three main choices for schooling: school at home, school at school, and school at home and school. Each choice considers the learning environment of the child, including the curriculum taught and their social environment.

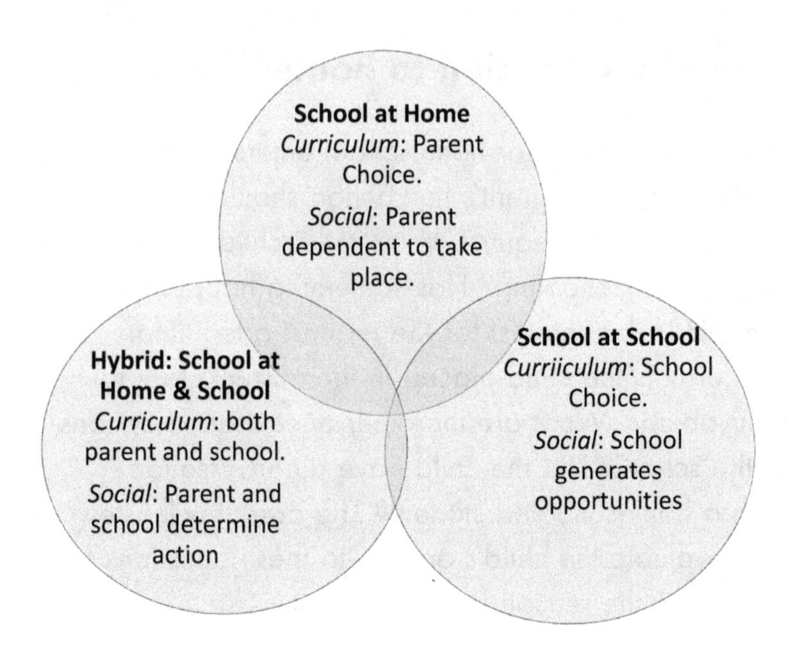

Curriculum choices and academic integrity

Regardless of the type of schooling chosen, there are important issues to consider around curriculum, socialization, and community resources. The curriculum selection at a public school is driven by state standards, school district textbook adoptions, and school-based ancillary materials. Private and charter schools have similar processes. These curricular choices are driven by factors such as cost, content, and perhaps politics. Some types of schools come with prescribed curricula like Montessori, Classical, religion-based, etc.

The homeschooling parent is given the responsibility of selecting their child's curriculum content and frequently pays the costs themselves. There is a plethora of websites, homeschool groups, and the testimonies of current homeschooling parents to help a parent decide what is best for their child. Several resources can be found at the end of this chapter. There is no "one-size-fits-all" curriculum for children.

The parent must research the options and select what works best for their child. Remember, many of these curriculum companies are for-profit. Check out the reviews of the curriculum on non-commercial or non-profit websites. Be alert to potential bias in the information.

There are curriculum choices which are totally online, partially online, and not at all online. These options are determined by the child's choice to be enrolled at a local school and take supplemental courses or if the child will take all their school courses at home.

Not all homeschooling happens in the home. There are groups formed of like-minded homeschooling parents that share the schooling experience. The formation of these groups is built upon similar curricula, the needs of busy parents, and the need for socialization. These types of schools are referred to as pod schools or micro schools and frequently hire a licensed teacher to conduct lessons. As with homeschooling, check the state guidelines for creating this type of school.

How does socialization fit into a homeschool environment?

How do I make friends?

When do I get to be in sports?

Will I be able to graduate?

Can I go to the community center during the school day?

I do not want to meet other kids my age.

Why can't we just stay home?

When do I get to see my friends who are still at school?

How are you going to teach me art because you can't draw a straight line?

These are all questions coming from the child who is, or will, be homeschooled.

Isolation is not part of the definition of homeschooling. Learning takes place in the home and in other learning environments. School systems are not replicated in the home. There are no bells, passing periods, rows of desks, homework cubbies, and lunch periods. The reason to learn at home is to break these barriers and learn as learning occurs. Some lessons may take an hour and others may take weeks.

Every community has occasions for socializing. It is up to the parent and the child how to proceed with these critical socializing opportunities. Check out what the child wants, needs, and must have in their social dynamic world. Shy and introverted children do not need to be forced into sports or community volunteer groups. A small and occasional learning group with children of their intellectual level may suffice. A savvy parent will observe and notice when groups need to be changed to benefit their child. Parents are advised to scaffold experiences toward the goal of developing a socially well-adjusted adult.

Remember, socialization is not defined as just being with similar people. Socialization gives the child tools to interact with persons different from themselves as well. Switching up environments is also important in acclimatizing children to the wider world and their future experiences.

Feeling connected to other people is more important than a calendar of social events. A child's feeling of loneliness can occur even in traditional schools. The peers of Smart Kids are often not their age. They have a difficult time relating to their own age group's interests or concerns. A homeschooled student may be given opportunities to gather with more relatable peers.

Parents should listen to their children and follow their interests and personality. A child does not have knowledge of community resources, so parents can provide choices and be present to make quick changes as necessary to keep their child happy, confident, and growing socially. This is one of the extraordinary benefits of homeschooling. The family can embrace the child for who they are and work to meet their individual needs.

Start looking... there is something out there for everyone

Time is a resource that can be controlled fully by the homeschooling family. The child may finish a lesson at record speed and seek intellectual stimulation from a different source. At other times, a project may go in an unexpected direction and last for weeks instead of the planned days. With the luxury of time, the homeschooler fits time to school, not school to time like traditional schools.

Socialization opportunities can easily be taken up with this control over the time of the homeschooler. Parents and their children can seek out social connections outside the home that are appropriate for the personality and needs of the child. The options range from homeschooler groups, to joining clubs, sports teams, paid work, and volunteering.

Hanging out with other homeschoolers. Check out the local homeschooling organizations through internet research. These gatherings are also good for parents to collaborate, pontificate, and gain support. The availability of internet resources and current school environments has encouraged the growth of homeschooling families. If one group does not fit, find another in the area that does fit.

Community and school-based sports teams. Many school districts have policies which allow homeschoolers to compete on their school teams. This is an opportunity for a child to socialize and compete with peers. If a homeschooler is preparing for a college scholarship in a sport, this is an important extracurricular activity to get started. Local organizations, such as the YMCA, also have youth sports teams for them to enjoy.

Youth organizations that match a child's interests. Extracurricular service organizations abound in every community. Research the national headquarters website to find a club in the local area. Examples of youth clubs include Cub Scouts, 4H, Boys and Girls Clubs, and YMCA. Examples of adult organizations with youth opportunities are the Rotary Club, Lions Club, Kiwanis Club, community theatre, and historical societies.

Giving back. Learning to serve others is a commendable activity with lifelong rewards. Match the volunteer opportunities with the child's interests, societal concerns, and talents. Examples of volunteering opportunities include food banks, tutoring, planting trees, trail maintenance, elderly visits, horse therapy, Teen Court, hospitals, Special Olympics, animal shelters, and Habitat for Humanity.

Get to work. A teen's first job is a true learning experience. Answering to a boss other than a parent is sure to stretch any child. Seek a job with hours that meet the homeschooling expectations of time. Most importantly, look for jobs that align with the child's personality and interests. An introvert may not enjoy work as a cashier, but library work would be a great match. Consider youth-oriented jobs.

Tip #17

How do I help my Smart Kid get ready for adulthood?

What is the value of a school administrator or teacher opinion of how to prepare a child for adulthood?

The answer is simple.

They have seen hundreds and even thousands of children enter their school or classroom and respond to the environment. This tip is a reflection of the opinions of school-based personnel, and is a baseline as each family has unique demands, stressors, and expectations. The ultimate goal is significant encouragement of active, focused support of a child into adulthood.

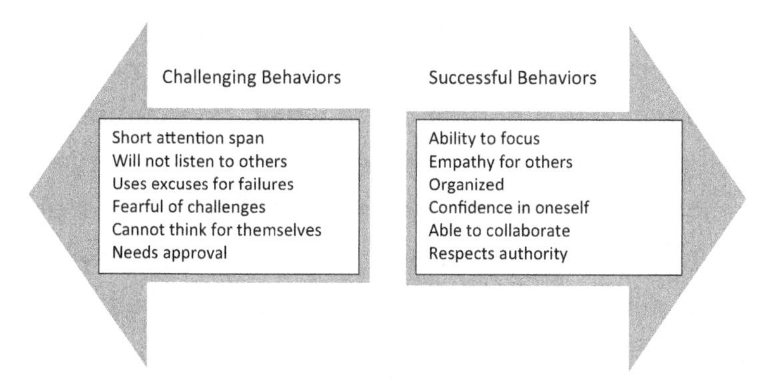

Common sense in preparing a child for adulthood

Be present. The child is on a path of constant physiological, intellectual, and emotional change. Blink and there will be a different child in front of you. Each year demands a different set of parenting skills. By spending time engaging with the child a parent can see and adapt to the change more successfully. The alternative is to be surprised by a change and overreact with a correction. Think about the adults in the child's life. The elementary-aged child spends between 5 and 7 hours a day with one teacher. The adolescent child will spend 45 to 90 minutes with each teacher. Can parents compete with that time? It's not likely and not necessary to compete. An active and interested present parent is invaluable.

Be trustworthy. Unreliability does not help in preparing a child to be a high-functioning adult, regardless of intent. Honoring commitments is a key pillar of raising a trusting adult. Think of a child's trust as a barrel of water. At the beginning of childhood, the child's trust confidently fills the barrel. Each broken promise removes a portion of the water. Each subsequent broken commitment removes exponentially more water. An empty barrel is a non-trusting child. Earning trust and replacing the water takes much longer. The memory of disappointment is much more vivid to a child than an apology, gift, or praise.

Avoid: Do what I say, not what I do. Modeling behavior has a stronger influence on a child's behavior than talking about it. Children are watching and judging. For example, if a parent wants a child to attend school on time, then their getting to work on time is a valuable model. Going to bed on time, researching questions with a reliable source, handling emotions, driving at the speed limit, conversational tones, even finishing a plate at dinner are all skills that can be modeled by a parent.

Ask the right questions in the right way. The opener is important. Starting with a judgmental phrase never works. Start with a sentence or two that covers common ground. Not every conversation needs to be a lesson. Enjoy the child's opinion. Verbally and publicly agree with them. Difficult correction conversations should start with the parent nudging the child to speak. These conversations need to be around 10% parent and 90% child. This is modeled in every school office. Most administrators know children do not learn from being lectured. Children excel at learning by exploring their own motivations. Show the child is appreciated and liked. This is a simple ask, yet oddly not valued in some parent–child exchanges. Effective communication starts with your physical presence. Then, it goes to the eyes. Remember, a conversation with a child will be influenced by all past communications, both positive and negative.

Limit cell phone exposure. The cell phone is an emotional being, not merely a communication device. If a parent believes the child is excessively using their cell phone, take steps to reduce time spent on it. Understand the habit of using the cell phone often is difficult to break. Parents should model responsible and limited use in front of their children. Conversations start with the explanation of why unlimited use is detrimental. Ask the child to create their own parameters. Talk it out. Negotiate. Give some flexibility. Teach why it is important. Don't just hammer home discipline – teach why it's important. Model the expectations to the child.

Notice changes. "I am OK" is often a lie. An astute parent notices changes in their child's behavior, attitude, or physical appearance. The child is always changing: their grade, size, knowledge, social situation, and even their family dynamics. Their resiliency wanes when the stress becomes overwhelming. Parents can get in front of challenging changes by predicting their child's response to a situation. This can only take place if the parent spends time with the child. Subtle differences are the warning signs. Look for signs of depression, bullying, drug use, etc. Start a calm yet productive conversation with the child to build trust. The Smart Kid will inform parents of their challenges if they trust the parent will be supportive, not judgmental or punitive.

Be unpredictable. The life of an adult is unpredictable. Both good and bad events can happen in an instant without warning. Give the child a taste of impromptu decision making. Offer fun opportunities without notice. Show up and participate unexpectedly. Keep this positive. Embarrassment is real and is to be avoided.

Family time is family time, not family-work time. Don't work on the family vacation. Model the nurturing of close relationships. A close family unit is grown with consistent actions that place the family before work or other distractions. A savvy child notices the adult's decisions during family time. The child's family priorities will mimic those of their parents.

Give responsibility. What is important to you? a clean room – no? This is why doors are made. Are the watching of siblings or cleaning the kitchen more important to the family? Other ideas: Keeping the family calendar up to date. Feeding the dog. Washing their clothes. Picking up siblings. Trash guy: gathering, taking out, and knowing which day to take the can to the curb. Finding support. Child one always puts out the drinks at dinner. Child two always sets the table. Child three always loads the dishwasher and completes the final cleaning of the kitchen. All others pick up their plates, rinse them and place them in the dishwasher.

Learn the value of mental breaks. Stopping and reflecting for a predetermined amount of time is a skill not often taught or valued by parents. The Smart Kid sometimes needs to clear their mind to help relieve the stress generated by high expectations. Preparing to be a well-adjusted adult includes practicing journaling, meditating, or simply taking a break to "chill" for a short time. This rejuvenation serves to reset the mind and create more effective and productive outcomes.

The importance of soft skills (character traits). The definition of a soft skill is the subjective ability to get along in a culture. Hard skills are those such as mathematics, language, fixing a car, etc. Parents are called on to train and teach their children the importance of these soft skills.

Soft skill examples					
Listening	Multitasking	Time management	Communication	Answering the phone	Punctuality
Organization	Patience	Answering the door	Handshakes	Asking for help	Remembering names
Creativity	Talking in a public place	Cultural acuity	Speaking in front of a group	Persuasion	Politely refusing
Greetings	Polite conversation	Judging a social situation	Respecting authority	Politely disagreeing	Saying thank you

Working a job. Working for a boss who is not a parent or educator is an excellent glimpse into adult life. The authority figure has control over schedules and pay. A good worker receives accolades and more resources. A job demands a Smart Kid show up on time, maintain a good work ethic, learn the job, and stay positive with fellow workers. The boss may make decisions which are not fair. Other workers may be less ethical. This exposure provides invaluable lessons and character development.

Volunteering. Often referred to as "giving back." A child has little to give but time, presence, work ethic, and their innocence of not knowing the world's challenges. By donating their time, a child has the potential to learn about people different from themselves. Serving underprivileged families gives them a real-world perspective of life outside the neighborhood. For example, donating time to planting trees in challenging environments teaches resiliency. The enjoyment and positive feelings of giving back can lead to a lifetime of service.

Getting away from home. Traveling to new places puts the senses into overdrive. There are new sights, sounds, food, accommodations, etc. Taking children outside of their home generates conversations that are unlikely to occur in the house. Turn off the technology or give predetermined and scheduled "tech time" during travels. Family travel time should be away from the routine distractions of school, work, and home. Keep conversations light and interesting. This is not a time to jump into controversial issues. Remember, part of the excitement of travel is preparing for the trip. Include the child in selecting the route, making packing lists, etc. These are life skills that will be useful as the child seeks more independence. Conversations about safety when traveling are important. Point out areas of concern such as loitering people, rest areas, talking with strangers, emergency preparedness, etc. Prior to arriving back at home, ask questions about what the child learned and enjoyed the most. Ask for specific details like the names of people, forts, cultures, towns, etc. This practice will prepare them for reporting back to friends and teachers.

No child is allowed to be disrespectful. Part of the preparation for becoming an adult is working on the skill to stop and think about the environment. All adults are to be respected regardless of the situation. This will be difficult for the child whose parents allow disrespect in the home. This does not mean the child cannot debate, disagree, or otherwise state their opinion. The skill is in the practice of communication which does not have an edge. Student–parent conferences and teacher-to-student conversations model these skills. Administrators are expected to call out a student's disrespect immediately if it occurs in front of parents, or any other adults.

Experiencing failure. "You mean I will not always win?" Smart Kids are prone to believe they can do anything – allowing a child to experience a challenge and fail at its completion sets them up for understanding their own limitations. Not trying something because of the high potential to fail is a negative trait. Allowing a child to fail and talking them through it prepares them with resiliency for similar situations in the future.

HACK

What does my child need to learn before they leave home?

1. How to do their own laundry from start to finish.
2. How to disagree with a stranger without making a scene.
3. How to eat a meal with polite habits.
4. When to keep their mouth closed.
5. That the internet is a public forum regardless of security precautions.

6. When to stop drinking, smoking, etc.
7. How to shake hands properly with eye contact.
8. How to solve a problem in a store.
9. How to solve a problem in an organization (school, bank, hospital, etc.)
10. How to read a map.
11. How to make an appointment with a doctor or another service.
12. What to do after a fender bender.
13. When to call a friend to take you home from a gathering.
14. The right opening words to get the desired outcome... from anyone.
15. When to let someone else win an argument.
16. How to change a light bulb, diaper, garbage bag, vacuum filter, and tire.
17. When a person is a scammer or a friend.
18. How to make and keep a budget.
19. The compounding danger of debt and credit cards.
20. What to say on a 911 call.

Tip #18

The "A syndrome" is real... watch out!

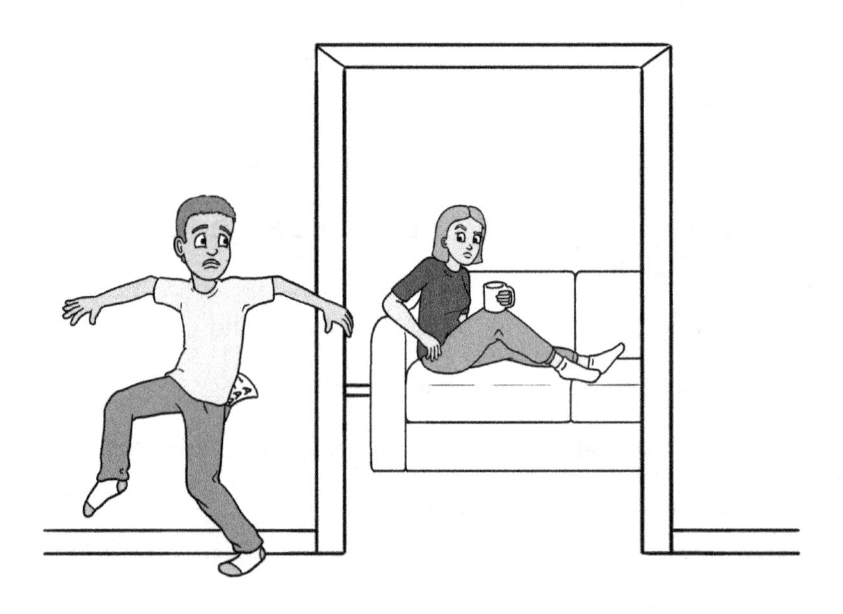

A child with "A syndrome" is commonly referred to as a "golden child." This is the description of the well-behaved and smart child who receives top grades and stays out of trouble at home and school. This child has earned this label by doing what is expected by the adults in their world.

Isn't this the type of child all parents are striving to bring up?

No! The child with "A syndrome" or the "golden child" is like other children, regardless of age or grade level. The only difference is their ability to adapt *with excellence* to the world of adult expectations. This tip reviews the different social and emotional layers of this child as seen in schools. Parents are given pointers to keep this child in balance with expectations and experiences.

Smart Kids have the ability to choose to be masters of "staying off the radar." Their parents have predictable responses and routines. It is not difficult for an astute child to discern how their behavior will impact a parent. Therefore, the child who wants to be left alone is adept at "staying off the radar" of their parents. The parents will not notice changes in their lives because the child does not want the parent to notice. Why?

The answer is simple:

> The parent has not earned their child's desire to have them as an active part of their life.

That answer is jarring to the parent who seeks a close relationship of trust with their child. There are frequent scenarios when a parent learns what is happening in a child's life during a student–parent conference. The child obviously has a different personality at school than in their home. The parent has accepted the child's good grades and behavior at home at face value and does not "rock the boat" with in-depth inquiries or substantial conversations about their life outside the home.

There is always *time* to delve into the child's world and explore what is revealed by the child. There are not always *opportunities*. It takes time to wait for the opportunity. Always show sincere interest, make observations of what both bothers and excites the child. Of course, all this will change with every year of growth. Punitive parental responses teach the child to find creative ways to keep their parents in the dark, if this is something the child wants to do again.

The following are two descriptions that illustrate two different "A syndrome" children. These scenarios were taken from real-life school experiences. You may recognize aspects of your child in one or both scenarios.

Scenario #1:

The Smart Kid is organized, has good grades, and is respectful to adults.

This child will have good friends and a larger circle of children of different ages for socializing. They frequently have leadership roles in school regardless of their age. They are trusted to run errands or answer questions correctly by their teachers. When they speak of problems, it is common that they have already determined the best solution. They ask for things infrequently and when they do it comes with explanations with reasoning. They guard their alone time to work on their organization, technology, and schoolwork. When a parent is allowed into this child's world there is little evidence of hidden agendas, underlying anxiety, or school-related issues. A parent may enter their space at home at any time. Their backpack, room, car, and desk are open for inspection.

Scenario #2:

The Smart Kid is organized, has good grades, and is respectful to adults.

This child has a few good friends. There is little talk about their friends, who tend to be non-communicative to you and to their own parents. This child spends hours alone and intensely guards this time. It is noticed that when a parent changes their routine or behavior, this child questions them about the change. This Smart Kid uses "buzzwords" they know will make the parent go away or stop questioning. They initiate few conversations with parents. The enjoyment of family time comes and goes. There is an expectation of privacy with their things, bedroom, closet, backpack, car, etc. This child encourages parents to leave them alone in the home.

How does a parent know which child is theirs? The outward behaviors are the same. Right?

It takes time to break down the barriers built by a "golden child" who is brilliantly adept at deflecting the attention of authority. Plus, the reasons for their overachievement may be parent driven. Is there pressure to always be the best? Does love and affection only come with a positive report from school? A child's opinion of themselves may reflect how their parents react to them when successes and failures occur.

The early years of the "A syndrome"

Knowing the intricacies of a child's life starts early in the parent–child relationship.

With infants, parents naturally maintain eye contact and give tactile approval. As a child grows this emotional connection should not change. A child's questions are received with praise and honest answers. The child's sentence structure is accepted regardless of their grammar or vocabulary. Constant correction slowly closes off communication due to fear of disapproval or embarrassment.

Listening is underrated. Repeating what a child says in the parent's own words is a communication method used by teachers and administrators. This rephrasing gives the child the chance to correct the message received by the adult and explain it in their own terms. Plus, this method models correct grammar, sentence structure, and vocabulary.

Wake up positive! The mornings are always exciting with the expectation of great things happening today. Daily conversations about the day's activities provide a routine that will gradually reveal a child's anxieties and hopes. Evening conversations have one purpose: take the stress out of that day. If the parent works to ensure safe, non-judgmental, and supportive conversations, then evening chats will build the relationship. This is when the child reviews the wild and crazy happenings at school.

Names are critical. Know the names of teachers, other school staff, friends, their parents, etc. Use the same name the child uses when appropriate. Ms. Brenda is a familiar name used by many children for me, not Dr. Small. If a coach is simply referred to as Coach, do not change this to her name. By using the same name, the parent sets a precedent of putting the child's vernacular before their own. If another child's name has not been discussed for a time, ask about the child. The answer may initiate conversations about friendship changes or a child moving to another school.

Who is that? Ask for descriptions of the children and people in the child's life. This can be their looks, actions, words, etc. There is the potential for bullying in every school. A parent will be one step ahead of this occurring if they know the names and behaviors of the people in the child's life. Understand the nuances of bullying behavior, because a child may not be aware of these negative behaviors themselves. Call it what it is: bullying. Give the child solutions to stop this behavior. Alert the teacher and administration about the bullying. There are statutes in every state that cover the required actions of a school when a child is being bullied or is accused of bullying.

Privacy issues increase as the child grows older. Maintain a precedent that the child's belongings are the family belongings. Privacy is respected yet must be earned. Set the precedent early that there is an open-door policy with the child's room. The computer is used in a common area. This is difficult to maintain when the Smart Kid's homework level increases. They will be less disturbed in their own room. However, take positive steps to keep the doors open and the screens facing the door.

The teen years of the "A syndrome"

If the parent has a child in the middle of their adolescence and late teen years, it takes a bit more of a delicate touch to gain transparency. A teen is not an adult, regardless of their level of discipline and responsibilities. Too often the "golden child" is given adult stresses to make their parents' lives more convenient.

Listen, listen, and then listen some more. There should be active listening taking place whenever the teen speaks. This is seen in nods, head shakes, laughter, concerned looks, questions about content, etc. Remember, a child will mimic their parents' use of a cell phone. If a parent is looking at a phone when the teen is speaking, the teen will do the same.

Notice everything. There is no occurrence that is too small; these may be an alert to something going on. New shoes. A new reading book. A scarf in their room that belongs to someone else. A need to go to school early. The conversation should be light and inquisitive, not blaming or punitive.

Get in there... be present at school and the child's extracurricular activities. Does anyone need a ride to practice? Those back seat conversations between children are invaluable for parents: it is a strange phenomenon that kids seem to forget an adult is in the car. A great time to sharpen your listening skills... avoiding eye contact will keep their conversation going. Show up unexpectedly at a practice or club event. Chat with the other parents. Make it seem natural and not like you're lurking.

Take a closer look. What book is the child reading? Pick it up and read it. Check it out online and ask about the characters. What is their "go to" website? What is the content? Do they converse with people online that they have not met? The computer's history? The content of the teen's conversations with other teens is compelling. Believe what you hear.

Birds of a feather flock together. Keep an open communication with teachers. They can compare the Smart Kid with hundreds and even thousands of other similar kids from their experience. Create a comfortable non-judgmental and non-threatening relationship with the child's teachers and/or the Gifted and Talented teacher. Keep communications private. The parent does NOT need to tell the student they are talking with their teachers. Make friends with the parents of your child's friends. Make this work. The time is invaluable. This is exceptionally valuable if the parent has only one child. Some parents with 3+ children are crazy smart when it comes to raising children.

Parenting a teen is just that, parenting. The job is not finished... yet. Furthermore, the parent with four children, the last of whom is an "A Syndrome" child, is also not finished parenting. Stay in the game. Children need their parents throughout their school years. This is the time when parents need to stay engaged in their child's life. Regardless of the age or behavior of the child, their parents are still needed. Period. There are no exceptions.

The Smart Kid's world is different

The child's success in school is a natural occurrence in most situations. Their motivations drive their work ethic and focus. They want good grades. If a student–parent conference is called, it is usually just a part of the school's routine. Discipline issues are rare. A higher maintenance sibling can take the focus off the Smart Kid who is "off the radar." Remember, compliance is not a reason to be an inactive parent. Give attention often.

Teachers need to feel comfortable alerting school leaders and parents of a change in a child's behavior. Often the Gifted and Talented specialist gets to know the child best because of their presence through the grade levels. Listen to the adults in the child's life. Gifted or accelerated programs cluster similar children. It is important for children to be with others with the same traits. This community serves to support a child's social, emotional, and academic needs.

The resources at the end of this chapter include topics on teen communication, violence, suicide, depression, etc. A Smart Kid needs savvy parents who are present and alert. Students do not always need solutions. They need safe environments to open up and discuss their opinions and fears.

Tip # 19

The importance of school choice, electives, and teachers

School choice can be so confusing!

The goal of schooling is to provide a child with experiences that facilitate their academic, social, and cultural growth. These lessons create a well-rounded thriving adult citizen. This is the baseline. Smart Kids need more. They need opportunities to extend their own learning and pursue their personal best.

In recent decades there has been an increase in opportunities for parents to select their child's school. This *choice movement* provides options beyond the neighborhood public school. The choices can be overwhelming. Public, private, magnet, charter, independent, pods, etc.: it's an exhausting list. Know, however, that there are no schools that are a perfect match for exactly what a child needs.

Parents start by reflecting on what is important to their family. Family values are a great place to start. Avoid listening to gossip about a school. It's out there about every school. One angry parent passing on their feelings does not mean the school isn't a match for other children.

Good questions parents ask themselves prior to researching schools:

1. What are the student's strengths and weaknesses?

2. How do they learn?

3. What is the desired relationship with staff (teacher, counselor, principal, etc.)?

4. Does the school have experience with your child's special needs? Explain.

5. I want to be involved in my child's education. What does that look like at your school?

Find a school that aligns with family values and a child's needs. Check out the school website. Keep an eye out for news items regarding academic accolades, sports, etc. Visit the school. Meet with the principal or other staff. "Feel" the culture of the school by visiting the front office, talking with staff and current students.

Good questions to start a conversation with school leadership:

1. Describe the student that thrives in your school and why?

2. How would the public describe your school?

3. Who is involved and how is the class curriculum selected?

4. What is your philosophy on educating Smart Kids?

5. Describe your teachers? What is their highest compliment of the school? Their biggest complaint?

6. Tell me about parental involvement at the school. What are the opportunities?

The accommodations given to Smart Kids vary by school, community, and state. Ask direct questions about the school's acceleration process. Dig into what they mean by support. This is a buzzword that has meanings varying from ability grouped classes, to pull-out programs, to simply setting accelerated assignments in each classroom.

School offerings

The needs of the Smart Kid are the lens to discern the adequacy of the school offerings. Is this a math kid? Then, look for course progressions in math that go up to the highest available in the state. Is the kid a literary person? Then, look for courses in poetry, literature, writing that go far beyond the basic secondary school curriculum.

Next, determine the programming and scheduling priorities in the school. This matters on many levels. Even a school's start time can be part of the reason for selecting it. Look for traditional, block, half day, virtual, and other models of class programming. Some schools even offer night classes. Accelerated academic programming can fit in any of the models. Listed below are the most popular of these:

✓ **Traditional:** each school day has periods 1 through 6, 7, or 8. These class periods are 45 to 60 minutes in length.

- ✓ **Block:** each school day has designated class periods. Periods 1, 3, and 5 meet on one day with 2, 4, and 6 meeting on the next day. Modified blocks incorporate a constant period which is usually the first or last period of the day. Blocks may rotate by day, or other models.
- ✓ **Half day with virtual or dual enrollment:** each school day has 2–3 periods assigned to each student at the school. The remainder of the day is for virtual learning on or off campus or for college-level courses through a dual enrollment model.
- ✓ **Optional:** schools may offer an optional period for two types of students: 1) Additional accelerated courses for college prep. 2) Courses needed to stay on track for graduation.

Smart Kids need accelerated courses to learn at the top of their learning level. Whether schools have built-in and available options for advanced learning is a key element of school choice. The students in these classes are intellectual peers. They need each other to boost their own learning through both support and competition.

Listed below are a few examples of accelerated options in secondary school:

- ✓ **Advanced placement** (AP) classes offered from 9th to 12th grade in various subjects. The company, College Board, writes these courses. The final assessments are normed, which means all students who take this course take the same test at the same time around the world. The results of a student's test give universities a strong understanding of the student's ability in that subject. Some universities offer college credit for AP courses. Average courses are valued at 1.0, honors at 1.5, and typically AP are valued at 2.0 for the GPA (Grade Point Average).

✓ **Dual enrollment** (DE) or **concurrent** classes are offered on or off the high school campus. College-endorsed teachers teach the college-level courses. The courses are usually offered as a replacement for high school courses. These are not normed classes. The college determines the course content and assessments. Some universities offer credit for DE courses.

✓ **Enrichment and acceleration** of the regular classroom curriculum is offered for high achievers. These assignments are determined by the teacher.

✓ **Honors classes** are available in multiple subjects. The content is accelerated. Most honors courses have a weighted Grade Point Average value of a 1.5. (Average courses are valued at 1.0. Honors at 1.5 and typically the AP is valued at 2.0.)

✓ **International Baccalaureate** is a competitive academic program of specific courses and assessments. Schools must apply and qualify and be evaluated every five years for this designation. Authorized schools offer accelerated curricula from kindergarten to 12th grade. The assessments for the courses are the same globally. They are taken on the same day and hour around the world. The assessment results provide universities with a strong understanding of a student's learning potential.

✓ **Credit by examination** is offered to students who display mastery in a subject or course. Advanced credit is offered for the course after successful completion of the examination. In general, this is the assessment used for independent study or internships.

✓ **Virtual learning courses** are offered as an option at a student's brick-and-mortar school to supplement the school's offerings. Or the school might be an all-online option. There are both public and non-public online school providers with a plethora of course options for students. Check out the list of online providers in the resources at the end of this chapter.

✓ **Residential and accelerated/honors** schools offer a highly selective and rigorous academic option for Smart Kids. There are opportunities for internships, mentorships, and advanced collegiate studies. Generally, students apply for admittance.

✓ **Early college** options are becoming more popular in the United States. Students take college-level courses which are applied to a college degree. Application for admittance is common.

✓ **Homeschooling** provides students with individualized education. There is a plethora of options for secondary homeschooled students to take supplemental or all high-level courses online or in person. Consider Advanced Placement, Dual (concurrent) Enrollment, and online providers. Most states welcome homeschooled students into the local school's clubs and athletics.

Elective choices impact the Smart Kid's life

Electives are required to graduate from high school. They have a specific purpose. Follow the reason for these electives by allowing a Smart Kid to select an elective that inspires them. Some students select electives to get a higher GPA. This is not encouraged.

Electives are the fun part of school. Parents should encourage Smart Kids to take a non-academic elective. This is a chance to mix with the less-academically minded students. There will be children in the class who are good at it... likely better than the Smart Kid. New friendships and respect for others can grow.

Combine a child's interests with a dynamic teacher and there is great potential to change a Smart Kid's future! An elective in medical skills can create a pre-med student. A robotics course has the capacity to inspire a future engineer. A business class might spark a student's entrepreneurial spirit. Electives can be a powerful part of the school experience.

Teachers matter!

Parents know that Smart Kids are purposeful when selecting an elective or non-elective teacher. Teachers make a difference, and they know it! The subject of a course can be less important than a dynamic teacher.

Here are some positive and negative factors that will form part of the Smart Kid's teacher choices:

Positives	**Negatives**
Fair grading practices	Difficult to earn an "A"
Homework is limited and relevant	Homework is busy work
Challenging problem-solving	No rigor, class is too easy
Sets group work during class	Irrelevant content to interests
Content is appealing to interests	No peers are in the class
More accelerated learners in class	Poor classroom management

Adapted from *Serving the Needs of Your Smart Kids* (Small, 2022a)

HACK

"Follow the money to the funding of Gifted and Talented."

Most states have partial or full funding of gifted education. These funds are allocated to school districts. The use of the funds is reported to the state and federal government. Some states have initiated voucher programs that make dollars available to parents to pay for education enrichment programs and in some cases a paid-for school choice. Conduct research to find funding allocated to teens or their individual needs. This valuable information will reflect the school, district, and state's commitment to Gifted and Talented education.

You can start with these resources from the Davidson Institute: www.accelerationinstitute.org/Resources/Policy/By_State/Default.aspx

Resources for further study

Fonseca, C. (2015). *Emotional intensity in gifted students: Helping kids cope with explosive feelings*. Prufrock Press.

Golden child syndrome impacts you from childhood through adulthood, say psychologists. www.womenshealthmag.com/life/a40314500/golden-child-syndrome/

Heilbronner, N. N. (2011). *10 things not to say to your gifted child*. Great Potential Press.

National Association of Gifted Children (NAGC). www.nagc.org/myths-about-gifted-students

Neihart, M. (2008). *Peak performance for smart kids: Strategies and tips for ensuring school success*. Prufrock Press.

Rivero, L. (2010). *A parent's guide to gifted teens: Living with intense and creative adolescents*. Great Potential Press.

Small, B. K. (2021). The global mindset of students, teachers, and school leaders. *Collegial Exchange, 88*(2).

Small, B. K. (2022a). *Serving the needs of your smart kids: How school leaders create a supportive school culture for the advanced learner*. Gifted Unlimited, LLC.

Small, B. K. (2022b). *Smart kid terminology: 25 terms to help gifted learners see themselves and find success*. Routledge.

Webb, J. T., Gore, J. L., Amend, E. R., & DeVries, A. R. (2007). *A parent's guide to gifted children*. Great Potential Press.

RESOURCES FOR HOMESCHOOLING INFORMATION AND SUPPORT

Blogs for and about homeschooling. www.davidsongifted.org/resource-library/gifted-resources-guides/guides-for-homeschooling-gifted-children/

Hoagies' gifted education page includes a list of multiple homeschool curricula for a parent to research, evaluate and select. www.hoagiesgifted.org/homeschool_curricula.htm

Organizing the home school environment. www.davidsongifted.org/gifted-blog/tips-for-organizing-your-homeschool-space/

BOOKS ON HOMESCHOOLING

Creative Home Schooling: A Resource Guide for Smart Families by Lisa Rivero.

Educating your Gifted Child: How One Public School Teacher Embraced Homeschooling by Celi Trepanier and Sarah Wilson.

Family Matters: Why Homeschooling Makes Sense by David Guterson.

Forging Paths: Beyond Traditional Schooling by Wes Beach and Sarah Wilson.

From Homeschool to College and Work by Alison McKee.

SOFT SKILL RESOURCES

Asbari, M., Purwanto, A., Ong, F., Mustikasiwi, A., Maesaroh, S., Mustofa, M., Hutagalung, D., & Andriyani, Y. (2020). Impact of hard skills, soft skills and organizational culture: Lecturer innovation competencies as mediating. *EduPsyCouns: Journal of Education, Psychology and Counseling, 2*(1), 101–121.

Succi, C., & Canovi, M. (2020). Soft skills to enhance graduate employability: Comparing students and employers' perceptions. *Studies in Higher Education, 45*(9), 1834–1847.

Vasanthakumari, S. (2019). Soft skills and its application in workplace. *World Journal of Advanced Research and Reviews, 3*(2), 66–72.

MENTAL HEALTH RESOURCES

Centers for Disease Control and Prevention. Violence impacts teens' lives. www.cdc.gov/injury/features/teen-violence-impact/index.html

Cross, T. L., & Cross, J. R. (2021). *Suicide among gifted children and adolescents: Understanding the suicidal mind.* Routledge.

Freeman, J. (2013). *Gifted lives: What happens when gifted children grow up.* Routledge.

King, C. A., Arango, A., & Foster, C. E. (2018). Emerging trends in adolescent suicide prevention research. *Current Opinion in Psychology, 22,* 89–94.

Paludi, M. A. (Ed.). (2011). *The psychology of teen violence and victimization [2 volumes]* (Vol. 1). ABC-CLIO.

Pham, T. T. H., Pham, T. H., Nguyen, T. S., & Nguyen, T. M. N. (2021). Family-based intervention for suicide prevention in adolescences: A systematic review. *Tạp chí Khoa học Điều dưỡng, 4*(1), 98–114.

Routt, G., & Anderson, L. (2014). *Adolescent violence in the home: Restorative approaches to building healthy, respectful family relationships.* Routledge.

Runcan, R. (2020). Suicide in adolescence: A review of literature. *Revista de Asistenta Sociala, 3,* 109–120.

Subramanian, M. (2014). *Bullying: The ultimate teen guide* (Vol. 38). Rowman & Littlefield.

Webb, J., Meckstroth, E., & Tolan, S. (2020). *Guiding the gifted child.* SCB Distributors.

Youth.Gov is a United States Government website designed to provide youth support. https://youth.gov/youth-topics/youth-suicide-prevention

Chapter 4

Villages Are Loud and Supportive

DOI: 10.4324/9781003332817-4

Tip #20

Describe your Smart Kid

Most parents believe their Smart Kid is special. This is a uniquely brilliant child with stunning attributes. Stories are expressed praising early walking, reading, and talking. All are true and heartfelt. This proud lens is an integral part of the family dynamic.

An enlightening exercise for parents is to describe their Smart Kid

Why is this important?

This process of actively describing their child clearly reveals the parent's opinion. By verbalizing or writing a description, the parent is forced to examine their views and judgments about their child.

These thoughts and opinions impact the *affective* side of parenting. In other words, a parent's opinion impacts their decisions and attitudes. Parents of high-level learners often experience a rollercoaster of emotions. Their child may be academically brilliant yet cannot keep their room clean or find their toothbrush. Procrastination may be their way of organizing their time and intellectual energy, but is often misinterpreted as laziness.

It is a factual understatement to say a Smart Kid is complex

Exploring a parent's description of their child leads them to more information to make better decisions. The answers provide parents with a starting point for casual and non-stressful conversations. Additionally, ask the child to describe themselves; the information discovered from this exercise will be invaluable in determining their intrinsic motivations and any causes for alarm.

The parent's description of a child is often different from teachers, school administrators, coaches, and counselors. *Why does a child have a different personality for each environment?* This is their choice, and their reasoning may be complex when confronted. These differences do not create positive and effective solutions in meeting the needs of children. It takes patient and prolonged communication to find the reasons behind these choices. Unfortunately, many of these differences are instead noticed and then addressed in rushed school conferences or in quick chats with other parents.

Teachers are unique in their ability to describe children. Ask each teacher to complete the *Describe This Smart Kid* questionnaire below. Their wisdom is derived from a vast data set of young people. When these experiences are bundled together and analyzed, the result will be the knowledge of what the child needs to succeed. The communication of clarity in a child's description starts with generating trust with a child's teacher.

Review the questions below. Ask the people in the child's support system (at school, a religious institution, their coach, and at home) to do the same. The Smart Kid should also fill out the questionnaire. It only takes a few minutes to gather the information needed to make better decisions.

By asking for at least five items in the descriptions, the person answering must dig into their personal opinions. Listing two or three is too easy; it is likely the final descriptors that have the most importance. If the list is completed verbally, watch out for changes in answers based on the interviewer's reactions. A written description avoids the impact of another person's behavior during the assessment.

Describe This Smart Kid	
1	Describe any attribute (positive or negative) of the child in five descriptive words.
2	Describe five social attributes/traits/behaviors of the child in a complete sentence for each of the five descriptive words.
3	List five academic strengths of the child.
4	What is the child's opinion of themselves?
5	What is the child's one greatest weakness at this age?
6	What is the child's one greatest strength at this age?
7	List five of the child's friends' names and a description of each.
8	What is the child thinking in your class/home/etc.? Be intuitive, make a guess based on their behavior and facial expressions.
9	What changes have you noticed in this child in the last 12 months? In the last two years?
10	Who is the child's model/hero/mentor who influences their thoughts and actions?
11	What are the child's five most precious items?
12	How would the child describe their parents/caretakers?

Are parents' perspectives always accurate?

Parents only know what their child wants them to know. This is a skill developed throughout childhood and perfected in adolescence. Often, children keep information from parents because they want to have it to themselves. This is not a slight on the parent. It is a choice made to exercise independence.

It is critical for parents to know negative or harmful information. It is not unusual for the school staff to have information that the parent does not. This is a tightrope. Each situation is considered independently in terms of the student's safety and parental responsibilities. Ask direct questions of school personnel. Ensure their answers are coming from direct knowledge and aren't a generalization.

School staff should listen to parents' insights about their child. And it is equally important for parents to listen to how teachers see the child. This may not be comfortable, but parents must hear it and add any new information to their perspective. Gather information from persons in the child's life prior to making any judgment calls.

Let me tell you who I am!

Ask a gifted child how they are different from others their age and they will list a plethora of positive and negative traits. Keeping these traits in mind is paramount in nurturing the best from a Smart Kid. The child's completion of the 12 *Describe My Smart Kid* questions can be a start for further conversations.

Look for clues in the child's social and emotional journey. Is there struggle? Determine if their "monsters" are real or imagined. This is an important role of the parent of a Smart Kid. Their uniquely high intelligence can create problems that may be minor to others or easily solved with pragmatic action. These "monsters" might be deadlines, other children, decisions about the future, athletic challenges, looks from others, perceived attitudes of others, grades, etc. The list can be endless for Smart Kids.

The answers to the questions will change each year of a child's life. Keep the tradition of asking the child to complete the 12 questions each year. Make it a fun activity the family completes at the same time. Select a time when everyone is getting along and there are no obvious stressors occurring in the home or at school.

HACK

Talk out the issues step-by-step using imagery. This technique is for any age level from elementary to post-graduation. It releases anxiety and takes the power out of the monsters. Verbally walk through the steps of the situation.

For example, a child is nervous about a big high-stakes test.

- ✓ Start with describing the morning breakfast and what they will wear.
- ✓ Move to the car or bus ride to school.
- ✓ Examine the room of the test and "feel" where the child will sit.
- ✓ "Look" at the test and the pencil with the child.
- ✓ "Watch" as others finish the test.
- ✓ Talk about the after party or recess planned to celebrate the completion of the test.

Tip #21

Find your tribe!

"Is there anyone out there the same as my unique Smart Kid?"

The Oxford definition of a tribe is a social group linked by social similarities with a common culture, character, interest, and language. The Smart Kid's tribe consists of other Smart Kids. This term is stronger than simply describing a social group. Smart Kids *need* and *understand* each other. They perform at their highest ability and are the most socially and emotionally stable when together. There are few exceptions.

A tribe is calling your child. Listen! Push them toward their tribe

As the number one survival skill for the maturing adolescent, finding like-minded people to share ideas, explore learning, and spend time with is critical. These are little "gangs" of Smart Kids who may be judged by those not accepted into their group. Yes, they speak differently and about strange subjects. Listen to them. They are thriving and growing together.

Watch as students seek out those similar to themselves. This is their comfort-zone. It is human nature to seek out those who think similarly. This strengthens the positive socialization of children who may be living through drama and angst each day.

Interestingly, there is seldom discrimination in a Smart Kid tribe. There is no difference in race, gender, religion, disability, or even age. It only takes intellect to join. They speak the same Smart Kid "language" regardless of their spoken language. Their common quest to learn more and discuss esoteric findings drives these friendships.

Parents should keep their Smart Kid's need of a tribe at the forefront when selecting schools. Ensure like-minded children are grouped together. It is a common practice to mix academic abilities within classrooms. This is often a benefit to the lower achieving students. However, it may be detrimental to the Smart Kid's academic growth. Ask the school how the students are grouped. Confirm that the high learning level is nurtured and not diluted into all mixed classes.

It is obvious to parents when their child finds their people. The excitement cascades into open dialogues about their new friends. The similarities are mentioned and celebrated. Such confidence is recognized and celebrated with these new relationships.

Gifted high school graduates attending the University of Pennsylvania filled out a survey asking them what benefited them most in their secondary experiences. They reported that being in a homogeneously (same) high-ability class fostered their growth. They found it was socially acceptable to enjoy learning and experienced a different way of thinking that gave them the opportunity to complete projects at their pace. These classes helped them to take academic risks and be comfortable with their own high intelligence (Peterson et al., 2012).

Parent power to encourage the Smart Kid to find their tribe	
1	Take notice of the child's friends. Call attention to how new members are entering the friendship circle and others are exiting the group. Open up a dialogue about the reasons.
2	Encourage the friends to spend time together by setting up opportunities at home or events related to their interests. Think about academic competitions, relevant movies, museums, space centers, robotics competitions, nature preserves, etc. Ask the group or their teacher for ideas.
3	Such events allow parents to talk. Encourage this communication. Troubleshoot school issues together. This is also the tribe of the parent. These can become powerful parent groups. Consider the changes needed in a school. Bring them to the administration as a group. Powerful!
4	Notice the "inter-tribe" competition. This common social structure propels the Smart Kid to strive to be the best in the group. There are no excuses accepted by peers.
5	Know when it is time to positively influence a change of tribe. Look for clues that the group is not a nurturing environment. Stay alert to the "culture" of the group and their activities.

What is the definition of a Smart Kid friendship?

Ask the child their definition of a "friend."

The answers will differ from the simple convenience of the neighborhood or family group. Of course, they want to be friends with people like themselves, who are similar in thought. Smart Kids look at similarities in intellectual and emotional maturity. This description may be outside of their grade level, age, or culture. Placing these like-minded individuals together facilitates their development and helps them form friendships.

When children are asked what they want most in their life, it is often a good friend. This feeling of being with a person in their tribe sets the emotional geography of their day. Their daily experiences are affected by the presence and the absence of friends (Silverman, 1993). These are powerful bonds with the potential to last a lifetime.

Teachers are a starting point for parents to inquire about who has similar characteristics in a classroom. A child may have mentioned a few names of children similar to themselves in the class. Take this information to the teacher with a request to arrange groups with these children and their child when possible.

A real-life scenario from *Serving the Needs of Your Smart Kids*:

> **School leader speaks to 8th graders about her high-achieving high school:** "The most important choice you can make is to be with your people. These are other students who are motivated like you and will keep you afloat when you lose your way or get "tired" of trying. High school is no different from finding your people in middle school. You can still be with people like you. But wait, how

> will you feel when you are not the smartest person in the class? There will be many smart kids in your class. This will make you better. These are your people. They will understand you and your motivations."
> (Small, 2022a)

Know when to change tribes

How is the tribe working out for the Smart Kid? Parents should pay attention to the child's attitude, grades, use of their time, how they treat each other, etc. Are these traits acceptable and edifying the young group of scholars? Or… are there any concerns with negative traits infiltrating the tribe?

Parents can take action when needed to delicately influence a change of tribe. "Friend" is a powerful word. It is best not to ask the child to find different or better friends. Start the process of finding situations for the Smart Kid to meet members of a more appropriate tribe.

Proper placement is a key component to continuing personal acceleration in learning. As we saw in Chapter 2, Frog Pond Theory suggests that children in a mixed-ability group will only strive to be the smartest in the group, no more. If a child is placed in a group of average learners or lower learners, the Smart Kid will only try until they are at the top of "average." Yay for them, they can sit back and relish their own brilliance.

If a child is placed in a group of high-level learners, the Smart Kid has to try harder to get to the top. Competition keeps the mind focused on succeeding. Placement in the proper learning environment is critical for acceleration to occur.

Parents should stay alert to the tribe selected by the child or by school staff. Class placement is critical to a child's success. Having high achieving peers is the foundation for a child to feel comfortable with their personality and desire to learn.

Smart Kids are aware of the successes and failures of each member of their tribe. It is common for a member who is not succeeding to be slowly ostracized from the group. Watch for the signs. The child will change their routine, stop talking about these "friends" and want to spend time alone.

Tip #22

I have an Army of Support out there!

It is a common hope that all adults want the best for all children. It is best to believe this is true until proven otherwise. A positive attitude has a higher potential to bring positive results than a negative attitude. *Attract more bees with honey than vinegar.* Correct? With this in mind, if a family has had a negative experience in one school it is important to give the next school the benefit of the doubt. Start fresh with positive expectations.

The school personality is alive and well

The village, aka school, has its own dynamics of hierarchy, power, routines, territory, procedure, and policy. A parent walks into a school with an issue that needs to be addressed that day. What happens next is determined by the culture of the school. Two opposite reactions that reflect two different school cultures are as follows:

> *"Yes, we will take care of this immediately. I will contact _____. Please have a seat. It should only take a few minutes."*
>
> Or
>
> *"You must make an appointment with ______ first. They will determine if you can talk to the principal. She has next Tuesday at 10am open."*

The culture of each of these schools is obvious: one is service-minded and the other is authority-minded. The parent's method of engagement with the school must be different depending on the culture. The parent has the same problem yet must work within the personality of the school to achieve the desired end. This tip (as are all 25 tips) is written from a teacher and school administrator's point of view. This lens gives parents a view from the "other side" of a school's internal operations.

Where to go when the going gets tough

Starting with the line of authority, determine who is closest to the problem. Teacher, counselor, administrator, school district, and other parents are all in a child's Army of Support. A child's communication about an issue to a parent may have details not revealed by the child. A student–parent conference is not always needed. The parent wants to go to the source. Do it. Start with the person closest to the problem. Gather information. Determine if this person has the power to change the situation. If not, go to the next person in the line of authority, and so on. Once the situation is addressed and solved to the parent's satisfaction, be appreciative of the Army of Support. Because knowing children, there will be another situation to be addressed around the corner.

Remember the role of the parent in a school. Parents have one (or a few more within their family) child. Their fight is for their one child. Their focus is on their one child. Their support is for their one child. They are advocating for their family. This plea is important to recognize and keep in the forefront for those in the child's Army of Support. Never accept a negative response from school staff with the reason that they have all the other children in the school to consider. It is wise for a parent to keep solutions confidential if the authority changes the rules, procedures, or policies for their one child. This occasionally happens. Discretion is important in these situations.

The Teacher: In-person exchanges during school events are highly valued. Reach out and chat with the child's teacher at every opportunity. Clear communication via email, text, etc. is critical with teachers. Keep emails to three or four sentences. Ask direct questions. Find something to praise. Subjects are often confirming a child's claims, asking for an opinion on why a child has certain behaviors, clarifying the reason for a grade, explaining an absence, asking for consideration to make up work, etc. Be specific. Only keep the email string going for four to five replies. Send a handwritten Thank You note with your child to give to their teacher for their help (or any other reason). This makes a difference in the teacher's daily interactions with a child. Never be defensive, blaming, disparaging of other children or teachers, or compare anything to other schools. Work within the environment of the child where the teacher is the authority.

If a child has a Gifted designation, a special teacher will be assigned to provide support. Keep an open communication with this front-line teacher. They are a trained expert in high-level learners. Learn from their experiences. Ask tough questions about your child. This is your go-to person when addressing school issues. Start with this teacher who understands Smart Kids, then move up the ladder of authority until the issue is resolved.

The Counselor: School counselors are trained in the academic requirements for each grade level and children's emotional attributes. Their personalities and choices on how to service students lie on a wide spectrum from *"I will stop everything and work with this one student until the problem is solved"* to *"Follow the system established, I don't have time for special cases."* The same counselor may display both of these, depending on their daily workload. Of course, parents want their child to have the first type of counselor. But be aware that a counselor's greatest and most limited asset is time.

It is a fact that counselors spend most of their time on struggling learners. The high achievers are often "off the radar" as they are not normally in danger of failing. Consequently, the parents of a Smart Kid need to prime their relationship with the counselor. Their communication and support will ensure a good relationship. For example, a parent may share important information they discovered on a test prep offering or college admission change. This communication is short and to the point.

The *Army of Support* for the social and emotional welfare of a child resides in the counselor's office. This environment is frequently a soft place to land for students. The discussions are not privy to other students or even parents. A child's good relationship with a counselor is what is desired by parents. This is a trained professional with knowledge of the child's age group. Also, of all others in the Army of Support, the counselor is the most likely to provide truthful assessments of teachers, programs, school systems, etc. Ask questions regarding how to solve a problem, even if the counselor has no control over the issue. Their advice is usually student-centered and not school-centered.

The Administration: An appointment with a member of the school leadership team is not always necessary. An active school parent also has access to the leadership outside of the school day. Attending athletic or academic competitions provides casual face time with these decision makers. These short conversations are instrumental in changing school policies, procedures, staff, etc. Sometimes issues are better left off written electronic communication. Remember, public school emails are legally available to the public through information request procedures. However, if an amicable solution to a problem has not been reached with teachers and counselors, meeting the school leadership is the next step.

Never accept a NO from someone who cannot give a YES

The school administration has the power to change or adapt rules for an individual or groups of children.

Understand that this adaptation is considered outside the norm and must be appreciated. A kind request will be met with grace. An unkind request will be met with a quick statement of the rules and policies. It is important to note that a school leader does not have the power to change a child's grade. Grades are strictly the teacher's choice.

Parents should go to the top school leader for concerns regarding student or staff safety. A change in start times, types of programs offered, etc. are also all good subjects for leadership. Do not expect a teacher or other staff member to be immediately fired. Teachers are to be valued as they are becoming more and more difficult to find. A principal will take complaints about a teacher and use methods such as mentoring, professional development, and other influences to change behaviors or attitudes. Of course, reported safety concerns will be immediately investigated and have the potential to lead to immediate termination.

The School District: The boss's boss resides within the school district. Parents reach out to this high authority when all other avenues have been exhausted. An appointment with the authority over elementary, middle, or high schools will provide information about the system. These leaders will ask the parent what solutions were offered within the school. Be ready with the reason why these solutions were unacceptable. This is a time for facts, not subjective reasoning. Be specific in outlining the requested change and why it is necessary for your child.

Parents: Other parents with similar thoughts and beliefs can be a strong part of the Army of Support. This is especially true of parents who have older children. They have "been there, done that" and can advise based on their experience. So, finding your tribe is as important for parents as it is for children. Discuss where to go and what to ask in a school system when there is a concern. This will save time and effort, ensuring you approach the right people for a solution.

Parents have the ability and power to influence an entire school community. A squeaky wheel, gets heard, but the quest for change or information must be accomplished honorably. Research the issue and communicate with compassion. Every child needs a champion in their school. Many times, this is the administrator with a heart for Smart Kids. Or it could be the counselor or a specific teacher. Find the champion in the school. Nurture this relationship. This champion is a fellow general alongside the parent in the Army of Support.

HACK

"I think my kid has special needs."

The federal government provides these steps in creating an Individual Education Plan (IEP). Steps to an IEP:

- ✓ Child is identified with the possibility of needing special education or services related to an IEP.
- ✓ The child is evaluated for services.
- ✓ A team reviews the evaluation and eligibility is decided.
- ✓ When a child is eligible for services an IEP meeting is held, resulting in the writing of an IEP.
- ✓ Services are articulated to all people involved.
- ✓ Progress is measured, and the results of meetings are reported to the parents. IEPs are reviewed on an annual basis. The entire process may take weeks or months to complete.

Tip #23

A Smart Kid community? I am in!

Why do Smart Kids need to socialize in activities outside of a school environment?

The answer is simple.

First, these non-school activities give the child a different perspective of people and themselves. Community members see the child for who they are in the group, not as a student or the parent's child. It is common that a Smart Kid's school reputation starts in the early elementary years. By branching out to groups outside of school, the child can create a new and often different persona. This is a fresh start with new friends and new challenges.

Second, these activities broaden a child's self-image. Talents they did not realize they had may appear. The systematic nature of activities in schools often pigeonholes students into roles and responsibilities. By branching out into unfamiliar environments, a child can explore different talents and abilities.

Who knew my child was good with special needs children?

Watch as she leads a group on how to tutor elementary students.

This child is a gifted speaker but never volunteers to make presentations at school.

Whoever would've thought this child wrote poetry so eloquently?

He never leads groups at school but look at him organize this fundraiser for church.

Gifted teens may express themselves with a perfected eyeroll that sends the message they have seen it all. At the same time, they can be innovative, with unexpected accomplishments. Their excitement is obvious in their intricate explanations and hours spent on their newfound project. This zeal should be rewarded with parental support. These teens will thrive in a home that encourages "outside-of-the-box" thinking and activities.

The first steps of getting involved can be scary. There are new and different people in the room. Everyone seems to know each other. This is a "new kid" syndrome that will last through the first meeting. Encourage them to take advantage of this status and jump into learning how to be genuine in this new environment.

What is out there for my child?

Quality Gifted and Talented community programs exist in most areas. They are not always labeled as such and may be difficult to find. There is rarely a rush to let families know what is available for their children in communities. These organizations usually have few funds to publicize and spread their message. The hunt for quality organizations that fit a child's interests, or predicted interests, is important and often exhausting.

Start with a conversation with the child. What do they enjoy the most in school? What have they heard about that they may be interested to explore? What are their friends participating in outside of school? What activity is within the budget and schedule of the family?

There are often many volunteering opportunities in every community. Look up museums, afterschool programs, environmental clean ups, libraries, senior resident homes, and volunteer organization programs like United Way. Giving back is a rewarding adventure for teens.

There can be a multitude of enrichment opportunities in even the smallest communities. Socializing in these structured environments is a safe and nurturing experience for Smart Kids. These connections are made organically through like interests. Consider a summer residential program where the child's interests are embedded into the activities. The friendships developed in these programs are unique and last through the school year. Check out the Davidson Institute's list of a variety of programs in each state here: www.davidsongifted.org/gifted-blog/gifted-summer-programs-residential/

Clubs in a community may be a part of adult service clubs. These clubs include the Rotary Club, Kiwanis, the Lion's Club, etc. Each has a youth committee organized for service projects. Community chess clubs and mathematics clubs can be vibrant, with member demographics crossing the spectrums of age, race, and culture. A child will learn to play, win, and lose from a variety of types of people.

The arts also welcome students of all skill levels into their community theaters and orchestras.

Sports are an option for all children, even the most awkward Smart Kid. Consider martial arts or fencing. These are sports demanding an in depth thought process. Martial arts are tactical sports requiring an extensive knowledge and strategy. Plus, this is an individually mastered sport with immediate rewards.

If you build it, they will come

What if my child likes (*insert activity here*) and there are no organizations in my area? It is time to start building the club or activity for the child and others looking for similar experiences. Growing a community club is easier today with social media. Post the gathering on Facebook, Nextdoor, Instagram, Twitter, and anywhere else recommended by the child. Forming local groups brings together like-minded children. Also, importantly, parents now have a ready-made social group to seek support and friendships.

Steps to start a Smart Kid club		
1	Articulate the reason for the club	Share interests, serve community, compete in contests, etc.
2	Organizational structure: determine the governance needed	President, secretary, treasurer, communications, social, etc.
3	Determine the criteria for membership, if any	Age, grade, interest, geographical area, past experiences, etc.
4	Outline financial expectations	Dues collected, budget needs, bank accounts, responsibility for funds
5	Create a website for the club	Webmaster, content writer, updates, calendars, upcoming events, etc.
6	First meeting should be upbeat and well organized	Elect or appoint officers, establish meeting times, agree on the mission, etc.
7	Meeting activities determined	Large or small separate groups, set agendas, outcomes, etc.
8	Stay social	Check in with members, communicate often, meet expectations

Tip #24

That is the coolest smart person I know!

Appropriate role models cannot be over-emphasized for Smart Kids

The high-level learners tend to want to socialize with persons older than themselves. This is only because of common interests and an ability to communicate at a more mature level than with same-age peers. This person gets it. They understand the child's vernacular to the point of nurturing growth in their own learning. This understanding is often reached during the first conversation.

The adult who has a unique understanding of the child's interests also influences future vocations. The mentor's purpose is to provide a safe place for the child to explore and advance their interests in opportunities that exist outside the regular school setting. This is an adult lens spending time with a young budding talent. A mentor will push a child toward acceleration in their area of interest and proficiencies that could not occur in an educational environment.

The value of a mentorship goes beyond sharing interests and proficiencies with a like-minded adult. A child's self-esteem increases as they work together with their mentor. They also gain confidence in their own abilities and do not feel they must "hold back" their intelligence. A parent may notice an increase in the child's interest in school and socializing with their peers. This new positive emotional attitude is a product of a good nurturing mentor experience.

Selection of an appropriate adult mentor is in the hands of the parent. This "imprinting" can be created purposefully by savvy parents. The parent places the mentor in the child's path. First, know and respond to the child's unique interests. Second, seek out the correct mentor.

What type of learner will benefit from a mentorship?

The characteristics of a Smart Kid are important to consider when deciding on a mentor, or even when considering starting a mentorship. An extraordinarily shy child needs time to adapt to a new person. Mentor situations are set up with parents who ensure these are positive experiences. Listen to the child's opinion of the experiences following a meeting with the mentor. Change what is necessary to improve the child's experience.

In contrast, an outgoing child needs their parents to select a mentor with a similar energy level and excitement in their commonalities. Parents carefully monitor the activities and the relationship to intercede if the child appears to be overwhelming the mentor. Scheduling the mentor–child meetings is the most effective technique to safeguard the mentor's time and energy.

The following informative guide outlines a child's learning style and preferences. The information can be used to link the child's learning style with a potential mentor. Ask the child to fill out the chart in their own words. Give it to the mentor prior to their first meeting. The chart can be a conversation starter between the parent and mentor. The mentor may use this information to ask the child what they meant by their answers.

Matching the traits of a Smart Kid to potential mentors

How do I think?	*Who am I?*	*How do I learn?*	*What am I into?*
My thinking process is beyond my same-age peers. I jump ahead of the teacher's lesson at times. I can analyze information.	I do not need to be told to do my work. I want to learn. I focus on learning what I want to learn. I learn from reading and experiencing information.	I am open to learning from new people. I pick up information quicker than my peers. I enjoy exploring new information.	My interests tend to cluster into one or two subjects. I move on to different interests. I am intense when I want to learn more about my interests.
Above average intelligence. Strong desire to achieve. Strengths in knowing how they learn. Strengths in working with others. A stickler for details. Frustrated with busy work. Respects, but will challenge authority with known facts. Irritated with incompetence in adults and peers.	Independent thinker. Does not need to be told what to do and when to do it. Pursues own interests without nudging from adults. Open to the personalities, needs and strengths of others. Enjoys learning new things. Is OK with learning they are incorrect. Focused learning is intense at times.	Learns from multiple delivery methods: lecture, project-based learning, exploration, discussions, etc. Enjoys fast-paced learning. Thrives on problem solving. Comfortable working in groups as the leader and as the non-leader. Open to learning from younger and older people.	Takes a subject and jumps in with both feet to learn all facets of the subject. Ability to transition to different subjects of focus. Usually focuses on one academic area like mathematics, science, technology, or language. Ability to adapt prior knowledge to current focus. Spends hours on one subject.

Adapted from Rogers (2002)

Who is out there to mentor my child?

The mentors of Smart Kids may not be in the family or school. Remember the goals of establishing a mentorship for the child. First, Smart Kids feel different from their peers. The mentorship provides a like-minded person. Second, parents want the child to learn from the mentor. This demands a mentor that is respected by the child as a person.

Look for mentors from diverse sources. The obvious mentors in a school are not necessarily the best fit for your child. The list below is written to stimulate ideas of possible mentors. It is not intended to be exhaustive.

- College professors
- Undergraduate students
- High school students
- School administrators
- Entrepreneur groups
- Government officials
- Doctors
- Attorneys
- Retired military personnel
- Grandparents
- Older siblings
- Church leaders
- Neighbors
- Coaches
- Professionals

Mentors are often much older and have common interests in vocations or hobbies. Parents will know they selected the correct mentor by the reaction of their child. This is a glimpse into what a child, especially a teen, is really like when experiencing a true peer. Stand back and watch as the child shows genuine excitement about their experiences. This exceedingly positive experience can have a profound influence on a child's development.

A true peer is the perfect mentor. The child will feel a camaraderie in this intellectual connection. There is no need to water down their conversation to be understood. Their intelligence is celebrated and not covered up with a quest to avoid being different. The pace is set by their mentor and themselves with no need to wait for others to catch up.

Monitoring the mentorship

It is obvious that placing children with an adult mentor requires the watchful eye of a parent. Check grades and evaluate how they are affected by the time spent with the mentor. Evaluate the project completion status and determine if the schedule of meetings needs tweaking for more or less time together.

Ask the child direct questions regarding their experiences. What have they learned from their mentor? What would they change about anything if they could? As the Smart Kid to describe the mentor in their own words. What do they talk about with the mentor? Is the time spent with the mentor valuable or wasteful? Do they want a different mentor? If so, why, and what are the different traits desired in the next mentor?

HACK

State and national examples of programs to research in your area:

ACE Mentor Program

Check & Connect

Dell Scholars Program

FFAC National High School Mentorship

First Scholarship Program

GE-Reagan Foundation Scholar Program

Give Something Back

MENTOR

Mentor Foundation Career Mentoring Program

Oliver Scholars

SkillsUSA

TeamMates Mentoring

Tip #25

It takes a village to raise Smart Kids!

"Who is in my corner? I would like support in raising my Smart Kid."

This is an acknowledgement that raising Smart Kids is challenging. There are resources to help all parents. Yet, the unique characteristics of high-level learners demand different strategies of motivation and support. Thankfully, the information is out there. With just a few steps, a parent can find answers along with the camaraderie of parents with similar children.

The capacity of a parent to use their village to stay informed is in their hands. Smart Kids and all children are moving targets. They change every year, moving along their own maturity journey. Parents know their children may be one step ahead of them most of the time, and they must work hard to keep up. It takes tenacity to keep the world of a child nurturing while staying alert to possible threats, but their village can help.

The village is filled with willing and competent support as expressed in previous tips: mentors, fellow parents, the tribe, gifted specialists, and mental health specialists. This tip pulls together ideas for additional support. So,

Who is in the Smart Kid village?

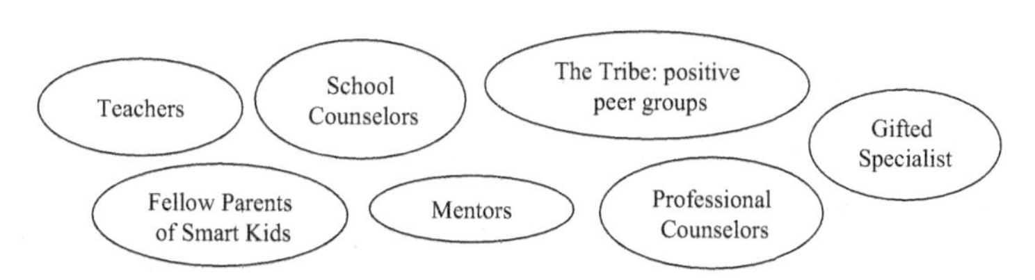

Teachers make a difference

Teachers spend hours with their students. This time is often more than the time kids spend with their parents. Depending on the academic schedule, teachers can spend between two and six hours with a student daily. These relationships are critical to a child's development. They have the power to be a positive or detrimental influence.

A positive motivating teacher with knowledge of how to teach Smart Kids is an incredible asset. A great teacher discovers how a child learns and meets these needs. Caring teachers follow their instincts on the social and emotional issues occurring in the lives of their students. Listen to the teachers' assessment of your Smart Kid. Welcome their input. Build a relationship of trust with this key member of the Smart Kid's village.

Effective Smart Kid teaching skills:

1. Student-centered in teaching approach, not content-centered.
2. Interested in the motivations and behaviors of each student.
3. Predictable and systematic in their classroom approach.
4. Interested in the cultural life of their community of high achievers.
5. Drawn to teaching for the student's intellectual growth.

6. Not intimidated by their students' high intelligence.
7. Have a desire to motivate students to want to learn and think independently.
8. Create a stimulating and imaginative classroom meant to stretch young minds.
9. Knowledgeable of teaching children with asynchronistic characteristics.
10. Well-grounded in their subject and enthusiastic about teaching it.

School counselors are in the village to offer help when needed

The role of the school counselor varies little within schools. They are the gatekeepers of information, academic choices, mental health support, etc. Their knowledge and experiences are powerful. In fact, their time is their greatest and most limited resource. With just a few computers clicks they can change the life of a Smart Kid. So, be nice to all counselors, all the time.

Generally, the top priority of counselors is to provide classes and support to all children to ensure they promote to the next grade level or to graduation. The Smart Kid is often left out of critical one-to-one appointments because they are expected to excel on their own. Their needs are just as important as a struggling student.

The past decade has brought more responsibilities into the counselor office. Their jobs have grown into redundant layers of state and national accountability tasks. Still, most counselors want to be that "soft place to land" for their students.

Parents, as well as their children, should work toward creating a positive relationship with the school counselor. A complete knowledge of what a counselor has the power to change is important when asking for assistance. These duties may vary between schools and assignments.

What counselors do	What counselors do not do
Change schedules with the right motivation	Change a schedule so a student can be in class with a friend
Help with university selection	Research individual university admission requirements
Help select classes	Keep secrets that may harm the student or others
First responder for mental health	Give parents information on other students or families
Keep what a student's says confidential, if there are no safety concerns	Determine what classes are needed for promotion or graduation

A student-centered school counselor is proactive in setting up successful situations for Smart Kids. They have the knowledge to assist a family in the exploration of different acceleration models. Individual exceptionalities can be communicated by a parent or the child to give the counselor information to directly serve the child's needs. They have the ability to select the best teacher or class for that child. Counselors always respond best to kindness.

The village contributors

A person's job or responsibility is not always defined as what is needed for a Smart Kid to thrive. Sometimes it is simply the right word spoken by someone who inspires, corrects, or otherwise leads the child into a more beneficial mindset. These conversations might occur at a grocery store, a movie theater, or a community event. The child will tell the parent. *"Guess what that man said?"* It is an epiphany to the adolescent. Go with it.

The members of the village in a child's life model personal qualities. These can be both good examples and poor examples. Keep conversations open about positive character, compassion, motivation, empathy, attitude, and even intelligence. The result is the child will have a better understanding of their own quest for self-improvement.

Discuss these topics one at a time when the Smart Kid is open to talking. Ask for details. No general answers should be accepted.

What are their *standards* for themselves?

What is *ambition*? How does it apply to them?

How and when are they *competitive*?

How do they describe their own ***ethics***?

When do they show *compassion* and why?

What is the cause of their self-motivation?

Parents have likely watched their Smart Kid take life very seriously and experience an over-sensitivity to an event. Surround the child with people who motivate yet are also quick to redirect a sensitive episode. A wise friend may say "Oh, let it roll off your back." Or a neighbor may be the one who expresses "That's just the small stuff, look at the big picture." Select mentors who respect a child's personality but also keep their childhood journey positive and productive.

A moment to discuss the self-care of the growing Smart Kid

Parents of Smart Kids agree that their world is complex. It is difficult to remember a childhood that experienced similar expectations. This is a different world now for the child than when parents were teens. The alert parent nurtures their child toward adulthood.

Schools are privy to a child's physical and emotional wellbeing. It is not difficult to assess a child and determine what is missing from their life. Staff will also notice the healthy and happy child who is thriving both emotionally and intellectually.

Take a moment to assess a Smart Kid within these topics. Reflect on the child, not a neighbor or friend of the child. Take this personally. Apply each item to the children in the parent's home.

1. Gets 7–9 hours of sleep each night.
2. Feels safe to open any conversation with a parent.
3. Feels safe to give a different opinion in the home.
4. Is able to break monotony by changing habits.
5. Has the ability to not study when it isn't needed to succeed.
6. Is allowed to listen to music while studying.
7. Often brings humor into the home.
8. Is given permission to not care about certain subjects or people.
9. Experiences patience from a parent or sibling.
10. Is allowed to find their own pace with project completion.
11. Is allowed to select their own focus.
12. Is given room to determine their own stress relievers.
13. Is given choices that are all beneficial.

14. Has the power to be their own person in thought and action.
15. Is allowed to think differently than authority figures.
16. Is provided with support for their unique ideas.
17. Is allowed to take a class or classes that will not appeal to a top university.
18. Is allowed to have friends who are not mainstream.
19. Is given room to make mistakes without hearing about them again and again.
20. Is allowed to find and enjoy their passions that may be perceived as odd.

Resources for further study

Blackburn, A. C., & Erickson, D. B. (1986). Predictable crises of the gifted student. *Journal of Counseling and Development, 64*(9), 552–555.

Davidson institute's list of a variety of programs in each state. www.davidsongifted.org/gifted-blog/gifted-summer-programs-residential/

Ford, D. M. (2011). *An action research inquiry into the relationship among aerobic activities, memory, and stress with students identified as gifted* (Doctoral dissertation). ProQuest Dissertations Publishing.

Lewis, B. A. (2009a). *The kid's guide to service projects: Over 500 service ideas for young people who want to make a difference.* Free Spirit Publishing.

Lewis, B. A. (2009b). *The kid's guide to social action: How to solve the social problems you choose-and turn creative thinking into positive action.* ReadHowYouWant.com.

National Association of Gifted Children. (2018). www.nagc.org/sites/default/files/Publication%20PHP/Sports%20that%20Work%20for%20Gifted%20Children%20March%202018%20PHP.pdf

Neihart, M., Pfeiffer, S. I., & Cross, T. L. (2016). *The social and emotional development of gifted children: What do we know?* Prufrock Press.

Palmer, D. (2011) Gifted kids with learning problems. *Psychology Today.* 12/26/2011. https://www

.psychologytoday.com/us/blog/gifted-kids/201112/gifted-kids-learning-problems?eml

Peterson, J., Canady, K., & Duncan, N. (2012). Positive life experiences: A qualitative, cross-sectional, longitudinal study of gifted graduates. *Journal for the Education of the Gifted, 35*(I), 81–99.

Reilly, J. (1992). When does a student really need a professional mentor? *Gifted Child Today Magazine, 15*(3), 2–8.

Rinn, A. N., & Wininger, S. R. (2007). Sports participation among academically gifted adolescents: Relationship to the multidimensional self-concept. *Journal for the Education of the Gifted, 31*(1), 35–56.

Rogers, K. B. (2002). *Re-forming gifted education: Matching the program to the child.* Great Potential Press, Inc.

Silverman, L. K. (1993). *Counseling the gifted and talented.* Love Publishing Co.

Small, B. K. (2022a). *Serving the needs of your smart kids: How school leaders create a supportive school culture for the advanced learner.* Gifted Unlimited, LLC.

Small, B. K. (2022b). *Smart kid terminology: 25 terms to help gifted learners see themselves and find success.* Routledge.

Tribe. (2022). In Oxford. www.oxfordlearnersdictionaries.com/us/definition/english/tribe

Chapter 5

The Wrap Up

The Complex Journey of Parenting Smart Kids

DOI: 10.4324/9781003332817-5

Parents and their child's school have an ability to be partners in the long game of raising children toward becoming adulthood superstars. This is a difficult journey. The needs of both the parent and the Smart Kid change each school year.

So, how is it going? It is going great with the applied 25 tips!

A wise and informed parent will bring in all their resources during this complex journey. These 25 tips are based on years of experience with thousands of students, mostly teens from 11 to 18 years old. If one of the 25 tips isn't applicable, wait a few years or even until the end of the week, and it may well appear as relevant to the parenting journey. And of course, these 25 tips can benefit children of all intellectual abilities and ages.

Remember that applying new family practices takes time and patience. Routines are difficult to break in a home and at school. Be ready for the push back. Remain steadfast with perseverance, and with your goals and affection for your child.

Remain aware that a maturing child may look at the world differently every morning during adolescence. Notice the changes in your child. There are "tells" in their behavior that can alert parents to investigate.

Sometimes Smart Kid behaviors are simply odd

Learn to love the child for *who* they are and *where* they are in their development. It is always a good reminder that the parenting journey continues daily. Build a community of strength. Stay open-minded and listen to both experts and the child.

Many children experience asynchronous development (when a person has different talents at different times). Child development is just that: *development.* Changes occur on a constant basis. Stay alert, aware, and supportive of these changes as they occur.

Comparing a child's past success when they fail is not endorsed. They are experiencing physical, mental, and emotional changes at all times. Their past talents grow into different talents. Celebrate who they are in the present. Find something they are good at and emphasize it.

The student-centered school administrator's viewpoint is significant

A teen's actions within a school reveal their experience of their journey through these final years they live with their parents. A savvy teacher, administrator, and parent have the capacity to work together to build a challenging and appropriate environment for learning, as well as maturing.

This occurs in many schools every day. Success takes an open mindset from everyone in the Army of Support.

Powerful parenting within a school system requires an eye for what is needed and the strength to make it happen. Work side-by-side with the school team to bring the best resources to the Smart Kid. Capitalize on the team's knowledge and passion to serve students. Know when to push and when to pull the team together to make changes. Be positive and supportive!

Many smart kids graduate from high school and attend university, but never reach their full potential, or even scratch the surface. An active and informed parent can make decisions to encourage their teen to grow into a well-rounded adult who thrives in their happy life as a productive member of society.

Share and explore

This resource has no value to parents if it's sitting on a shelf. Take the time to share these 25 tips with friends, other parents, counselors, school administrators, teachers, children, and every advocate in the Smart Kid's life. Bring up one of the tips and start a conversation. This is the time to "cuss and discuss" what is accepted and applied and what is not. This is where true collaboration and growth in understanding starts. So, talk about it!

Explore the Resources at the end of Chapters 2, 3, and 4 to further study how to serve your child. Look up these resources, explore the content, learn more about each subject. All are accessible on the internet. Knowledge is power. Never stop learning about how to serve a Smart Kid. These resources feed the exploration journey. Everyone has an opinion. Find what fits.

About the Author

Dr. Brenda Kay Small is currently a university professor, author, speaker, and education consultant. She is the founder of Lead Smart Education, LLC, an education firm dedicated to teaching, researching, and spreading the word of the importance of serving all children at their learning level at home and in schools.

As an educator for over 22 years in multiple states, Dr. Brenda Kay Small's leadership experiences reach beyond schools and into communities through the mentoring and teaching of future school leaders, and developing unique partnerships with both community organizations and business leaders. She teaches master's- and doctoral-level education leadership courses and enjoys the challenge of writing current and meaningful graduate-level education leadership course curricula.

She uses her opportunities as a guest speaker, presenter, and author to spread the news on how and why to build supportive cultures in student-centered environments.

Her books are written to inspire and spread the word of how to better serve high-level learners. She believes the Smart Kid is the nation's most precious natural resource. Her books bring her experience to life with positive actions to inspire parents, students, school leaders, teachers, and community advocates. *Smart Kid Terminology: 25 Terms to Help Gifted Learners See Themselves and Find Success* gives readers illustrated terms describing Smart Kid traits. Her successful educational leadership experiences are provided in *Serving the Needs of Smart Kids: How School Leaders Create a Supportive School Culture for the Advanced Learner* for readers to use to create school environments designed to support high-level learners.

Dr. Small earned the Administrator of the Year Award for her work in building schoolwide career academies that prepare all levels of students for post-secondary success. As a classroom teacher, she received the Florida Social Science Teacher of the Year Award, and the Florida Excellence in Teaching Award.

Her doctorate and master's degrees were earned from the University of South Florida in Education Leadership and Policy Studies. A true westerner, Dr. Small and her family enjoy living in her home state of Colorado.

Learn more from Dr. Small on her website: leadsmarteducation.com. Sign up for her newsletter and read her blog for current conversations on serving children in the nation's schools. Professional coaching for teachers and administrators through online trainings brings the message to thousands of educators. Parents are invited to participate in online seminars related to bringing the best to their children.

Illustrations by Holly Brogaard

Printed in the United States
by Baker & Taylor Publisher Services